ROUTLEDGE LIBRARY EDITIONS: PERSIA

Volume 4

'OMAR KHAYYÁM

'OMAR KHAYYÁM

The Persian Text with Paraphrase, and the First and Fourth Editions of Fitzgerald's Translation

E. H. RODWELL

Routledge
Taylor & Francis Group

LONDON AND NEW YORK

First published in 1931 by Kegan Paul, Trench, Trubner & Co., Ltd.

This edition first published in 2018
by Routledge
2 Park Square, Milton Park, Abingdon, Oxon OX14 4RN

and by Routledge
711 Third Avenue, New York, NY 10017

Routledge is an imprint of the Taylor & Francis Group, an informa business

© 1931 Kegan Paul, Trench, Trubner & Co., Ltd.

British Library Cataloguing in Publication Data
A catalogue record for this book is available from the British Library

ISBN: 978-1-138-05482-0 (Set)
ISBN: 978-1-315-11348-7 (Set) (ebk)
ISBN: 978-1-138-05938-2 (Volume 4) (hbk)
ISBN: 978-1-138-06106-4 (Volume 4) (pbk)
ISBN: 978-1-315-16268-3 (Volume 4) (ebk)

Publisher's Note
The publisher has gone to great lengths to ensure the quality of this reprint but points out that some imperfections in the original copies may be apparent.

Disclaimer
The publisher has made every effort to trace copyright holders and would welcome correspondence from those they have been unable to trace.

'OMAR KHAYYÁM

عمر خيّام

Persice
'Umar-i-Khayyám

THE PERSIAN TEXT WITH PARAPHRASE, AND THE FIRST
AND FOURTH EDITIONS OF FITZGERALD'S TRANSLATION

BY

Brigadier-General E. H. RODWELL, C.B.,
I.A. (ret.)

LONDON
KEGAN PAUL, TRENCH, TRUBNER & CO., LTD.
BROADWAY HOUSE: 68–74 CARTER LANE, E.C.
1931

ERRATA

p. vi, l. 14.   *For* Rubá'iyat *read* Rubá'iyát.

p. 36, l. 2.   The last word should be ‏کرد‎.

p. 52, last quatrain.   *For* ‏ماد‎ *read* ‏ماه‎.

Printed in Great Britain by Stephen Austin & Sons, Ltd., Hertford.

PREFACE

THIS little work has no extravagant pretensions. Its aim is merely in a simple, sound, and lucid manner to show how the genius of two poets ('Omar Khayyám and FitzGerald) brought together by the genius of an Orientalist (Professor Cowell) culminated in a very strange, very beautiful, and profound English poem. It is in a way an extension of Mr. Heron-Allen's admirable work. But whereas Mr. Heron-Allen dealt with the sources of FitzGerald's inspiration, this little book is concerned in addition with the actual genuineness of the verses ascribed to 'Omar Khayyám. Moreover, if I may say so, it goes further than Mr. Heron-Allen's work, for it deals with quatrains that are peculiar to FitzGerald's 1st edition, and includes in its purview both the 1st and 4th editions. It is founded, too, on MSS. that were not available to Mr. Heron-Allen, or not scrutinized with the same intent, and it deals with criticism from what was formerly St. Petersburg, from Copenhagen, and from Berlin, that is quite modern.

No Persian scholar can read Mr. Heron-Allen's surpassing elaboration without wondering to what extent the Persian quatrains represent the genuine production of 'Omar Khayyám's genius. This is the problem that chiefly confronts us. If we cannot solve it with certainty we can at least take a long stride forward towards its solution.

But before entering further on this interesting question let us remember that FitzGerald's paraphrase (though he himself makes use of the word "translation") was not and never pretended to be a mere translation of the Persian text. It is much more—a very full and highly poetic rendering of the essence of 'Omar's speculations on the transitoriness of man on this globe, and of his consequent philosophy of life ; and whereas 'Omar expressed himself in separate verses, or epigrams, of four lines each, FitzGerald welded selected verses with consummate skill into a connected poem.

Writing to Professor Cowell on 3rd September, 1857, he explained :—

" My translation will interest you from its form, and also in many respects in its detail ; very unliteral as it is. Many quatrains are smashed together, and something lost, I doubt, of Omar's simplicity, which is so much a virtue in him." [1]

This being the case there is, I think, room for a metrical translation that shall keep close to the original and give at once, and in short space, an idea of what the words of the original mean. No one would be so foolish as to compete with a master such as FitzGerald, but however much we admire and acclaim the players who in a wider field with brilliant runs and great *tours de force* carry the

---

[1] See *The Works of Edward FitzGerald*, Macmillan, 1903.

ball towards the goal, there is still room for those whose rôle is to keep " on the ball " ; and great and gallant ships " that plough the main " are not without " tenders " ; and if indeed my verses should serve merely as a foil to set forth more clearly the beauty of FitzGerald's quatrains, they will not serve in vain. But for those who would go more deeply into the matter a literal translation is provided which, eschewing any attempt at style and phrasing, gives an accurate rendering of the original.

FitzGerald's introduction and his notes are given in full. But it is to be remarked that his biographical note on 'Omar Khayyám and his friendship with two school companions is in the present day held to be apocryphal. Dr. Fr. Rosen writes :—

" Although this tale has been proved to be a myth by E. G. Browne, Sir Denison Ross, Professor A. Christensen, and other scholars, it recurs in every one of the countless editions of the Rubá'iyat and may live as long as 'Omar's immortal verses." [1]

I have added some notes. If, like a boy, I have wandered on the shores of the immense sea of Persian literature, and if I have perchance picked up here and there a shell or pebble, it is indeed a small matter if I also show them to my playmates.

To revert now to the question of genuineness. We shall be on firm ground if we go to Dr. Rosen for an explanation of this question as it presents itself to the experts. Dr. Rosen, writing in the *Zeitschrift der Deutschen Morgenländischen Gesellschaft* in 1926, re-states the argument that is familiar to those who have read Whinfield's work. I venture to translate :—

" The Oxford MS. contains 158 quatrains, while the number of verses in most of the later collections is substantially higher. Speaking generally we may say that in proportion as a collection is more modern the number of quatrains contained in it is greater. Modern lithographed Teheran editions contain more than one thousand verses. We may estimate as nearly five thousand all the quatrains ascribed to 'Omar. From this it appears that in course of time many interpolations of spurious verses must have taken place. It is exceedingly difficult to decide how many out of this mass of verses really belong to 'Omar and how many should be considered as later additions. It has been stated that the number of genuine quatrains amounts to about 250 or 300."

Here we find the argument of 1883 repeated in 1926 with augmented force, for the number of quatrains ascribed to 'Omar is brought up to nearly 5,000 !

I naturally hesitate to question this statement, and yet I am inclined to think that the number of " replicas " or " family " quatrains has been greatly

---

[1] See Dr. Rosen's *Quatrains of 'Omar Khayyám*, Methuen, London, 1930.

exaggerated, that the number of genuine quatrains might be put at twice the number here given, and that the number of quatrains ascribed to 'Omar might be halved.

This argument seems to have been founded on the assumption that 'Omar, as we may say, " signed, sealed, and delivered " his own edition, and the experts, or some of them, devoutly hope that some day the original version will be discovered. But let us look at the facts. We see in the present day the same process of augmentation. The Calcutta printed version of 1836 had fifty-four quatrains added to it from a note-book. The Lucknow version of 1924 has eight more quatrains than that of 1878, and Dr. Rosen has himself printed a Persian version of 329 quatrains and added in the same volume (1) a version written by Sultán Muhammad Núr, containing sixty-three quatrains, and (2) a version written by Muhammad Bin Badr-i-Jájarmi containing thirteen quatrains. We may reasonably think that in the past different collections have tended to flow together.

Now we know that in ancient times it was the custom for the learned to meet together in order to recite verses of their own composition and perhaps to drink wine, or possibly to drink first and recite afterwards, and some of 'Omar's verses refer to this very custom. There is therefore good reason to think that 'Omar's quatrains were in all probability given out at these meetings, that they were copied, perhaps, but certainly treasured in the memories of his friends, and that after his death they were collected, just as the Kurán was collected, " from the mouths," to use an Oriental expression, of the people.

This is merely a theory, but it would account for the phenomena that obtain, phenomena common to ballads.

Let us again see what Dr. Rosen has to say on this subject. Towards the end of his most learned and most interesting article we find (my translation) :—

" The poetry that has been handed down to us from 'Omar appears to have never been collected during his life-time into a diwán or any similar collection. The strict orthodoxy that prevailed under Nizám-ul-Mulk in Naishápúr,[1] and confronts us in this statesman's ' record of penalties ', would have made this difficult. We must suppose that 'Omar gave out, as he was able, separate quatrains to the intimate circle of his friends, perhaps at re-unions like those in Balkh, which 'Arúzi has described as *majlis-i-'aish* or drinking bouts ; that these verses then circulated from mouth to mouth and very soon found imitators. Later, probably after the murder of Nizám-ul-Mulk, 'Omar's verses may have been recorded and collected, whence the spurious may have been adopted with the genuine."

---

[1] Not Nishapur as Dr. Rosen writes and as is shown in most maps. As I have explained elsewhere, my old Persian friend objected most strongly against the name of this town being pronounced " Nishapur ". FitzGerald has the name correctly.

If this theory is correct the best way of obtaining readings that shall be as nearly genuine as possible would seem to consist in comparing the readings from different sources and adopting as our text those that are identical. *This is what I have done* ; and I need scarcely say how agreeably surprised I was last June (when through the kindness of Dr. Rosen his article in the *Zeitschrift der Deutschen Morgenländischen Gesellschaft* came into my hands) to find that the theory on which I had been working for so long was so amply endorsed by his great authority.

As to modern criticism, it may be worth while to state the views of Professor M. Mahfuz-ul Haq, M.A., who writes : " A curious thing about these copies (referring to the Amritsar version) is that " new " quatrains of 'Omar which are discovered in old MSS. and anthologies—say in Jájarmis' *Munis-ul Ahrar*—are also present in these copies, so we cannot possibly reject or condemn these uncritical editions. The discovery of new MSS. of 'Omar is rather enhancing the value of these uncritical editions, as we find that quatrains which were considered as ' not genuine ', as they were found in these uncritical editions only, are found in newly-discovered old codexes also. Hence such editions have a value of their own."

This preface has perforce run to greater length than is desirable, but the principles on which my work is based need explanation. They are :—

(i) That the comparison of different readings should embrace *original documents* or copies of such documents only.

(ii) That consequently all " selections " by European and American scholars should be excluded.

(iii) That differences that are insignificant and do not affect the sense should not be taken into account, on the legal principle " de minimis non curat lex ".

(iv) That for brevity's sake verses that suffer from misprints, copyist's errors, etc.,[1] should simply have the word " defective " put against them.

A list of MSS. and other documents consulted is attached as an appendix to this preface.

It remains now to express my thanks to all those who have helped me :—

To Sir Wolseley Haig, M.A., K.C.I.E., C.M.G., C.S.I., C.B.E., who helped me in some difficult passages. Some of his notes will be found in square brackets.

To Sir E. Denison Ross, C.I.E., Ph.D., who read over my translations and gave me the good advice " *to read everything I could get hold of* ".

To Mr. Heron-Allen, who with the utmost generosity placed " all his studies at my disposal ".

---

[1] Dr. Rosen writes : " Nicht selten kommen falsche Lesungen vor und selbst Fehler, *welche den sinn entstellen.*" My italics.—E. H. R.

To Dr. Fr. Rosen, who supplied me with his very remarkable article in the *Zeitschrift der Deutschen Morgenländischen Gesellschaft*, and who gave me authority to quote from his learned works.

To Professor M. Mahfuz-ul Haq, the Presidency College, Calcutta, who has helped me with his criticism and in other ways.

To Messrs. Macmillan and Co., Ltd., for their great kindness in allowing me to use the fourth (copyright) edition of FitzGerald's translation.

Lastly, and not least, to the memory of Mirza Ibrahim Muhammad of Shiráz who read Persian poetry with me, wrote much poetry himself under the " takhallus " of " Fáni " or " Mortal ", and has now these very many years put on " immortality ".

E. H. RODWELL.

Holbrook,
> Near Ipswich.
> *29th October*, 1930.

APPENDIX I

O. This letter stands for

(*a*) The Ouseley MS. No. 140, in the Bodleian Library, Oxford, written at Shiráz by Shaikh Mahmúd-i-Jarbúdaki in the year A.H. 865 = A.D. 1460/61. It contains 158 quatrains.

The authority of this version is strengthened by the discovery of an identical copy. Professor M. Mahfuz-ul Haq writes : " The Lahore MS. is in possession of Khwája Md. Salim, M.A., a landlord of the place. The copy is exactly identical with the Ouseley MS. It was transcribed by Hajji Farajullah in Baghdád in 868/ 1463–4. There are 143 Rubá'iyát. Of these 135 are identical with the Ouseley copy. I enclose a copy of the ' 8 ' quatrains that are absent from the Ouseley MS."

(*b*) Professor Cowell's copy of the above. No. " Add 4510 " in the University Library, Cambridge. Professor Cowell's note is as follows :—

" This is the copy which I made from my own transcript of the Bodleian MS. of 'Omar Khayyám in Sir W. Ouseley's collection and gave to FitzGerald in June, 1856. We were both staying at my mother's house at Rushmere, near Ipswich, before I went to India. I read the Persian with him (I had only recently discovered the MS. at Oxford). This transcript first introduced 'Omar to his future translator. It came back to me after my friend's death."

(Initialled E. B. C.)

C. This letter stands for the copy of the MS. formerly in the Bengal Asiatic Society's Library at Calcutta, referring to which Professor Cowell, writing to Mr. Heron-Allen, says :—

" I got a copy made for him (FitzGerald) soon after I arrived in November, 1856. It reached FitzGerald June 14th, 1857."

Through Mr. Heron-Allen's kindness I am enabled to quote it from his works. The original was lost or stolen, and a copy made for Professor Cowell (by him put at Mr. Heron-Allen's disposal) was the only record left of this MS., which was known as No. 1548 in the Library above mentioned. It contained 516 quatrains.

C¹. This symbol stands for

(*a*) The Calcutta printed edition of 1836 which is in the Library of the India Office, London. It is bound up with "Vernacular Tracts, Persian" and numbered 103. It contains 438 quatrains and has an appendix of 54 quatrains in addition. Referring to this edition, Professor Cowell says :—

"Some time after this (after his arrival in Calcutta E.H.R.) I sent him, Fitz-Gerald, a copy of that rare Calcutta printed edition which I got from my Munshi."

(*b*) A copy of the above-mentioned book which bears the inscription : "A copy of the Calcutta old printed edn. made for me in Calcutta," initialled E. B. C. This is O. R. 262 of the Cowell Bequest in the Cambridge University Library.

Mr. Heron-Allen states that "this edition is evidently printed from the lost Calcutta MS. itself, both introduction and quatrains being identical in readings and sequence"; but I may be allowed to remark that a close scrutiny shows that in the quatrains with which we are concerned, omitting differences due to errors in script and to misprints, eleven quatrains have been slightly altered, and five quatrains radically altered, and one quatrain omitted.[1]

B stands for MS. O. R. 10,910 in the British Museum, a highly illuminated MS. of Háfiz with the quatrains of 'Omar Khayyám inscribed within blue flowered brackets with ground-work of gold at the beginning of each ode. The script is Nast'alik. The leaves are still powdered with gold dust and at the end are two much battered pictures of hunting scenes. The MS. is undated, but is said to be of the sixteenth century. The number of quatrains is 460, including one or two duplicates.

B¹ stands for MS. O. R. 5966 of the British Museum, dated A.D. 1569 (script Nast'alik), containing 269 quatrains.

B¹¹ stands for MS. O. R. 331 of the British Museum. The script minute Nast'alik—the diacritical marks often wanting. The whole book so small as to fit easily into a waistcoat pocket. Dated A.D. 1623, contains 545 quatrains.

B¹¹¹ stands for MS. O. R. 5011 of the British Museum. Dated A.D. 1668, contains 400 quatrains.

B¹¹¹¹ stands for MS. O. R. 330 of the British Museum ; eighteenth century, contains 423 quatrains.

Bye stands for MS. 367 of the Bodleian Library, presented by the Rev. Theodatus Bye, of Maidstone, in 1760 ; no dates, but probably sixteenth century ; contains 405 quatrains.

Ca stands for a MS. in the Cambridge University Library. A note on the fly-leaf states that the volume containing the MS. formerly belonged to the Nawáb of the Carnatic, whose seal is said to be on the first leaf of the text. The seal reads "Muhammad Ali Husain Khán" and bears the date A.H. 1210 = A.D. 1795. The script is a very closely written Shikasta. Is said to contain over 800 quatrains. Cf. Whinfield, pp. xv and xviii. Probably eighteenth century.

I stands for MS. 906 in the India Office Library. Dated 1811, contains 512 quatrains.

I¹ stands for MS. 907 in the India Office Library. No date, not identical in quatrains common to it and to 906 (above) as might be inferred from the label ; contains 362 quatrains.

L stands for the Lucknow lithograph of the Nawal Kishor Press, 1878. Has a likeness to "Ca" above ; contains 762 quatrains, many defective.

---

[1] The following have been slightly altered : 44, 85, 95, 143, 156, 159, 201, 286, 297, 396, 641. The following have been radically altered : 110, 273, 281, 314, 431. No. 510 is not in the printed text.—E. H. R.

L¹ stands for the Lucknow lithograph of the Nawal Kishor Press, 1924. Has many alterations from the edition of 1878, and gives in a short preface a quite needless prominence to two very blasphemous quatrains which it is quite certain 'Omar Khayyám never wrote, for, as Dr. Rosen points out, had he done so they would certainly have been used against him by his enemy, Najmuddin Rázi. The result of the alterations in the text is to bring it nearer to that of " Bye " ; from which we may assume that " Bye " is a copy of some well-known version ; contains 770 quatrains.

N stands for a reprint of a Teheran version, published as *Les Quatrains de Khèyam* by J. B. Nicolas in the Imperial Press, Paris, 1867. It is a very beautiful piece of work, and such as is rarely seen in the present day. It deals with 'Omar Khayyám exclusively from the point of view of modern Sufism. Was used by Edward FitzGerald in his variations and additions subsequent to his first edition ; and specially for two quatrains 46 and 98, 4th edition.

P stands for the MS. in the Bibliothèque Nationale, Paris, Ancien Fonds, No. 349, ff. 181–210. Dated A.H. 920 = A.D. 1514 ; a very beautiful MS. in the Nast'alik script, containing 213 quatrains.

P¹ stands for the MS. in the Bibliothèque Nationale, Paris, Supplèment Persan, No. 823, ff. 92–113, dated A.H. 934 = A.D. 1527, in the Nast'alik script, containing 349 quatrains.

P¹¹ stands for the MS. in the Bibliothèque Nationale, Paris, Supplèment Persan, No. 826, ff. 391–4. Dated A.H. 937 = A.D. 1530 in the Shikasta script, containing 76 quatrains.

P¹¹¹ stands for the MS. collection of poems, fol. 104, Supplèment Persan in the Bibliothèque Nationale, Paris, in the handwriting of the eleventh century of the Hijrah, containing 8 quatrains.

P¹¹¹¹ stands for the MS. collection of poems in the Bibliothèque Nationale, Paris, Supplèment Persan, No. 1417, dated A.H. 879, a very beautiful, highly illuminated MS. in the Nast'alik script. It commences with the same apologetic or propitiatory quatrains as the Ouseley version, and many quatrains are the same as in that version ; contains 258 quatrains.

P¹¹¹¹¹ stands for MS. Supplèment Persan, No. 1481, in the Bibliothèque Nationale, Paris, a small collection of favourite quatrains. The verses are pasted into illuminated borders on Chinese (?) paper, which is shaded in yellow and covered with life-like pictures of fighting animals, trees, etc. Probably sixteenth century A.D. ; contains 31 quatrains.

R stands for a reprint of a MS. in private possession, discovered by Dr. Fr. Rosen, and published by him in 1925 (Káviáni Press, Berlin) The date given in the MS. is A.H. 721 = A.D. 1321, but the Nast'alik script forbids the idea that it was written so early. The original, of which Dr. Rosen's MS. is a copy, probably bore the date A.H. 721, and the copyist copied the date also. See Dr. Rosen's article in the *Zeitschrift der Deutschen Morgenländischen Gesellschaft*, 1926 ; contains 329 quatrains.

R¹ stands for a reprint of a MS. written by Sultán Muhammad Núr and dated A.H. 930 = A.D. 1523/24. Published by Dr. Rosen in the same volume as the MS. above (R) ; contains 63 quatrains.

R¹¹ stands for the oldest known collection, namely that written by the poet Muhammad Bin Badr-i-Jájarmi, reprinted by Dr. Rosen and published in the same volume as the two foregoing (R and R¹). The date is A.H. 741 = A.D. 1340/41 ; contains 13 quatrains.

T stands for Taqí Kashís *Khulásat-ul-Ash'ar* in the Oriental Public Library, Patna. The collection includes 16 quatrains of 'Omar Khayyam, ff. 390, 391.
See Professor M. Mahfuz-ul Haq's article in *Islamic Culture*, No. 3, 1929 (published at Hyderabad, Deccan.)

A stands for the Amritsar lithographed version, a collection for which Maulvie Imamuddin Sahib of Gujrat is responsible.   It is a very excellent piece of work, remarkably free from errors of penmanship, and the writing is bold and clear;   contains 924 quatrains.

W   stands for Mr. Whinfield's excellent, well-known and beautifully printed book, published by Trübner, London, 1883, containing 500 quatrains.   I endeavoured to get into communication with Mr. Whinfield, but without success.   Neither his quatrains nor his translation have in any way been consulted by me, but I thought that Mr. Whinfield would not object to my adding to the usefulness of my book by noting when he has dealt with parallel quatrains, and even noting in some cases the actual text with which his is in agreement.   His text is generally similar to N.

APPENDIX II

The references in the notes are to the following :—

Eastwick's Gulistán, 1850.
Háfiz, Haidari Press, Bombay, 1883.
The Korán, Rodwell's Translation, 1861.

EDWARD FITZGERALD'S INTRODUCTION

OMAR KHAYYÁM

THE ASTRONOMER-POET OF PERSIA

OMAR KHAYYÁM was born at Naishápúr in Khorassán in the latter half of our eleventh, and died within the first quarter of our twelfth, century.

The slender story of his life is curiously twined about that of two other very considerable figures in their time and country, one of whom tells the story of all three. This was Nizám ul Mulk, Vizyr to Alp Arslán the son, and Malik Shah the grandson, of Toghrul Beg the Tartar, who had wrested Persia from the feeble successor of Mahmúd the Great, and founded that Seljukian Dynasty which finally roused Europe into the Crusades. This Nizám ul Mulk, in his *Wasiyat*—or *Testament*—which he wrote and left as a memorial for future statesmen—relates the following, as quoted in the *Calcutta Review*, No. lix, from Mirkhond's *History of the Assassins*.

"'One of the greatest of the wise men of Khorassán was the Imám Mowaffak of Naishápúr, a man highly honoured and reverenced—may God rejoice his soul; his illustrious years exceeded eighty-five, and it was the universal belief that every boy who read the Koran or studied the traditions in his presence, would assuredly attain to honour and happiness. For this cause did my father send me from Tus to Naishápúr with Abd-us-Samad, the doctor of law, that I might employ myself in study and learning under the guidance of that illustrious teacher. Towards me he ever turned an eye of favour and kindness, and as his pupil I felt for him extreme affection and devotion, so that I passed four years in his service. When I first came there, I found two other pupils of mine own age newly arrived, Hakim Omar Khayyám and the ill-fated Ben Sabbáh. Both were endowed with sharpness of wit and the highest natural powers; and we three formed a close friendship together. When the Imám rose from his lectures, they used to join me, and we repeated to each other the lessons we had heard. Now Omar was a native of Naishápúr, while Hasan Ben Sabbáh's father was one Ali, a man of austere life and practice, but heretical in his creed and doctrine. One day Hasan said to me and to Khayyám: "It is a universal belief that the pupils of the Imám Mowaffak will attain to fortune. Now, even if we *all* do not attain thereto, without doubt one of us will; what then shall be our mutual pledge and bond?" We answered: "Be it what you please."—" Well," he said, " let us make a vow, that to whomsoever this fortune falls, he shall share it equally with the rest, and reserve no pre-eminence for himself." " Be it so," we both replied, and on those terms we mutually pledged our words. Years rolled on, and I went from Khorassán to Transoxiana, and wandered to Ghazni and Cabul ; and when I returned I was invested with office, and rose to be administrator of affairs during the Sultanate of Sultan Alp Arslán.'

" He goes on to state that years passed by, and both his old school-friends found him out, and came and claimed a share in his good fortune, according to the school-day vow. The Vizier was generous and kept his word. Hasan demanded a place in the government, which the Sultan granted at the Vizier's request ; but, discontented with a gradual rise, he plunged into the maze of intrigue of an Oriental Court, and, failing in a base attempt to supplant his benefactor, he was disgraced and fell. After many mishaps and wanderings, Hasan became the head of the Persian sect of the *Ismailians*—a party of fanatics who had long murmured in obscurity, but rose to an evil eminence under the guidance of his strong and evil will. In A.D. 1090 he seized the castle of Alamút in the province of Rúdbar, which lies in the mountainous tract south of the Caspian Sea ; and it was from this mountain home he obtained that evil celebrity among the Crusaders as the ' Old Man of the Mountains ', and spread terror through the Mohammedan world ; and it is yet disputed whether the word *assassin*, which they have left in the language of modern Europe as their dark memorial, is derived from the *hashish*, or opiate of hemp-leaves (the Indian *bhang*) with which they maddened themselves to the sullen pitch of Oriental desperation, or from the name of the founder of the dynasty, whom we have seen in his quiet collegiate, days at Naishápúr. One of the countless victims of the assassin's dagger was Nizám ul Mulk himself, the old school-boy friend.[1]

" Omar Khayyám also came to the Vizier to claim his share ; but not to ask for title or office. ' The greatest boon you can confer on me,' he said, ' is to let me live in a corner under the shadow of your fortune, to spread wide the advantages of Science, and pray for your long life and prosperity.' The Vizier tells us that when he found Omar was really sincere in his refusal, he pressed him no further, but granted him a yearly pension of 1,200 *mithkáls* of gold, from the treasury of Naishápúr.

" At Naishápúr thus lived and died Omar Khayyám, ' busied,' adds the Vizier, ' in winning knowledge of every kind, and especially in Astronomy, wherein he attained to a very high pre-eminence. Under the Sultanate of Malik Shah he came to Merv, and obtained great praise for his proficiency in science, and the Sultan showered favours upon him.'

" When Malik Shah determined to reform the calendar, Omar was one

---

[1] Some of Omar's Rubáiyát warn us of the danger of Greatness, the instability of Fortune, and while advocating charity to all men, recommending us to be too intimate with none. Attár makes Nizám ul Mulk use the very words of his friend Omar [Rub. xxviii]. " When Nizám ul Mulk was in the agony (of death) he said : ' Oh God ! I am passing away in the hand of the wind.' "

of the eight learned men employed to do it ; the result was the *Jaláli* era (so called from *Jalál-ud-din*, one of the King's names)—'a computation of time,' says Gibbon, 'which surpasses the Julian, and approaches the accuracy of the Gregorian style.' He is also the author of some astronomical tables, entitled ' Zíji-Malikshághí', and the French have lately re-published and translated an Arabic treatise of his on Algebra.

" His Takhallus or poetical name (Khayyám) signifies a tentmaker, and he is said to have at one time exercised that trade, perhaps before Nizám ul Mulk's generosity raised him to independence. Many Persian poets similarly derive their names from their occupations ; thus we have Attár, ' a druggist,' Assár, ' an oil presser,' etc.[1]

" Omar himself alludes to his name in the following whimsical lines :—

> ' Khayyám, who stitched the tents of science
> Has fallen in grief's furnace and been suddenly burned ;
> The shears of Fate have cut the tent ropes of his life,
> And the broker of Hope has sold him for nothing ! '

" We have only one more anecdote to give of his life, and that relates to the close ; it is told in the anonymous preface which is sometimes prefixed to his poems ; it has been printed in the Persian in the Appendix to Hyde's *Veterum Persarum Religio*, p. 499 ; and D'Herbelot alludes to it in his *Bibliothèque*, under *Khiam* [2] :—

" ' It is written in the chronicles of the ancients that this King of the Wise, Omar Khayyám, died at Naishápúr in the year of the Hegira 517 (A.D. 1123) ; in science he was unrivalled—the very paragon of his age. Khwájah Nizámi of Samarcand, who was one of his pupils, relates the following story : " I often used to hold conversations with my teacher, Omar Khayyám, in a garden ; and one day he said to me : ' My tomb shall be in a spot where the north wind may scatter roses over it.' I wondered at the words he spake, but I knew that his were no idle words.[3] Years after when I chanced to re-visit Naishápúr, I went to his final resting-place, and lo ! it was just outside a garden, and trees

---

[1] Though all these, like our Smiths, Archers, Millers, Fletchers, etc., may simply retain the surname of an hereditary calling.

[2] " Philosophe Musulman qui a vécu en Odeur de Sainteté dans sa Religion, vers la fin du premier et le commencement du second siècle," no part of which, except the " Philosophe ", can apply to our Khayyám.

[3] The rashness of the words, according to D'Herbelot, consisted in being so opposed to those in the Korán : " No man knows where he shall die." This story of Omar reminds me of another so naturally— and when one remembers how wide of his humble mark the noble sailor aimed—so pathetically told by Captain Cook—not by Doctor Hawkesworth—in his *Second Voyage* (i, 374). When leaving Ulietea, " Oreo's last request was for me to return. When he saw he could not obtain that promise, he asked the name of my *Marai* (burying place). As strange a question as this was, I hesitated not a moment to tell him ' Stepney ', the parish in which I live when in London. I was made to repeat it several times over till they could pronounce it ; and then ' Stepney Marai no Toote ' was echoed through an hundred mouths at once. I afterwards found the same question had been put to Mr. Forster by a man on shore ; but he gave a different and indeed more proper answer by saying : ' No man who used the sea could say where he should be buried.' "

laden with fruit stretched their boughs over the garden wall, and dropped their flowers upon his tomb, so that the stone was hidden under them." ' "

Thus far—without fear of trespass—from the *Calcutta Review*. The writer of it, on reading in India this story of Omar's grave, was reminded, he says, of Cicero's account of finding Archimedes' tomb at Syracuse, buried in grass and weeds. I think Thorwaldsen desired to have roses grow over him; a wish religiously fulfilled for him to the present day, I believe. However, to return to Omar.

Though the Sultan "shower'd favours upon him" Omar's epicurean audacity of thought and speech caused him to be regarded askance in his own time and country. He is said to have been especially hated and dreaded by the Súfis, whose practice he ridiculed, and whose faith amounts to little more than his own, when stripped of the mysticism and formal recognition of Islamism under which Omar would not hide. Their poets, including Háfiz, who are (with the exception of Firdausi) the most considerable in Persia, borrowed largely, indeed, of Omar's material, but turning it to a mystical use more convenient to themselves and the people they addressed; a people quite as quick of doubt as of belief; as keen of bodily sense as of intellectual; and delighting in a cloudy composition of both, in which they could float luxuriously between Heaven and Earth, and this world and the next, on the wings of a poetical expression, that might serve indifferently for either. Omar was too honest of heart as well as of head for this. Having failed (however mistakenly) of finding any Providence but Destiny, and any world but this, he set about making the most of it; preferring rather to soothe the soul through the senses into acquiescence with things as he saw them, than to perplex it with vain disquietude after what they *might* be. It has been seen, however, that his worldly ambition was not exorbitant; and he very likely takes a humorous or perverse pleasure in exalting the gratification of sense above that of the intellect, in which he must have taken great delight, although it failed to answer the questions in which he, in common with all men, was most vitally interested.

For whatever reason, however, Omar, as before said, has never been popular in his own country, and therefore has been but scantily transmitted abroad. The MSS. of his poems, mutilated beyond the average casualties of Oriental transcription, are so rare in the East as scarce to have reacht Westward at all, in spite of all the acquisitions of arms and science. There is no copy at the India House, none at the Bibliothèque Nationale of Paris. We know of but one in England: No. 140 of the Ouseley MSS. at the Bodleian,[1] written at Shiráz A.D. 1460. This contains but 158 Rubáiyát. One in the Asiatic Society's Library at Calcutta (of which we have a copy) contains (and yet incomplete) 516, though swelled to that by all kinds of repetition and corruption. So von Hammer

[1] Nevertheless at the time when this was written there was in the Bodleian Library No. 367 of the Oriental MSS. containing 405 quatrains, given to the Library about the year A.D. 1760 by the Rev. Theodatus Bye, of Maidstone.—E. H. R.

speaks of *his* copy as containing about 200, while Dr. Sprenger catalogues the Lucknow MS. at double that number.[1] The scribes, too, of the Oxford and Calcutta MSS. seem to do their work under a sort of protest ; each beginning with a tetrastich (whether genuine or not) taken out of its alphabetical order ; the Oxford with one of apology ; the Calcutta with one of expostulation, supposed (says a notice prefixed to the MS.) to have arisen from a dream in which Omar's mother asked about his future fate. It may be rendered thus :—

> " Oh Thou who burn'st in heart for those who burn
> In Hell, whose fires thyself shall feed in turn ;
> How long be crying, ' Mercy on them God ! '
> Why, who art Thou to teach, and He to learn ? "

The Bodleian quatrain pleads Pantheism by way of justification ; [2]

> " If I myself upon a looser creed
> Have loosely strung the Jewel of Good Deed,
> Let this one thing for my atonement plead :
> That One for Two I never did mis-read."

The reviewer,[3] to whom I owe the particulars of Omar's life, concludes his review by comparing him with Lucretius, both as to natural temper and genius, and as acted upon by the circumstances in which he lived. Both, indeed, were men of subtle, strong and cultivated intellect, fine imagination, and hearts passionate for truth and justice ; who justly revolted from their country's false religion, and false, or foolish, devotion to it ; but who fell short of replacing what they subverted by such better *hope* as others with no better revelation to guide them, had yet made a law to themselves. Lucretius, indeed, with such material as Epicurus furnished, satisfied himself with the theory of a vast machine fortuitously constructed, and acting by a law that implied no legislator ; and so composing himself into a stoical rather than epicurean severity of attitude, sat down to contemplate the mechanical drama of the universe which he was part actor in ; himself and all about him (as in his own sublime description of the Roman theatre) discoloured with the lurid reflex of the curtain suspended between the spectator and the sun. Omar, more desperate, or more careless of any so complicated system as resulted in nothing but hopeless necessity, flung his own genius and learning with a bitter or humorous jest into the general ruin which their insufficient glimpses only served to reveal ; and pretending sensual pleasure as the serious purpose of life, only *diverted* himself with speculative

---

[1] Since this paper was written (adds the Reviewer in a note) we have met with a copy of a very rare edition, printed at Calcutta in 1836. This contains 438 Tetrastichs, with an appendix containing 54 others, not found in some MSS.

[2] No task could be more distasteful than to point out lapses on the part of the poet, but even Homer is said to nod. There is, I think, no question of Pantheism here. The quatrain refers to the chief tenet of Islam, the unity of God, concerning which Sádi says : " A Musulman will suffer his head to be cut off by a sharp sword rather than deny the unity of God." The meaning is : " However slack I have been in worship, or obedience (*tá'at*) yet I hope for mercy as I have always held fast the doctrine of the One God."

[3] Professor Cowell.

problems of deity, destiny, matter and spirit, good and evil, and other such questions, easier to start than to run down, and the pursuit of which becomes a very weary sport at last !

With regard to the present translation. The original Rubáiyát (as, missing an Arabic guttural, these *tetrastichs* are more musically called) are independent stanzas, consisting each of four lines of equal, though varied, prosody ; sometimes *all* rhyming, but oftener (as here imitated) the third line a blank. Somewhat as in the Greek Alcaic, where the penultimate line seems to lift and suspend the wave that falls over in the last. As usual with such kind of Oriental verse, the Rubáiyát follow one another according to alphabetic rhyme—a strange succession of grave and gay. Those here selected are strung into something of an eclogue, with perhaps a less than equal proportion of the " Drink and make merry " which (genuine or not) recurs over-frequently in the original. Either way, the result is sad enough : saddest perhaps when most ostentatiously merry : more apt to move sorrow than anger toward the old tentmaker, who after vainly endeavouring to unshackle his steps from destiny, and to catch some authentic glimpse of To-morrow, fell back upon To-day (which has outlasted so many to-morrows !) as the only ground he had got to stand upon, however momentarily slipping from under his feet.

While the second edition of the version of Omar was preparing, Monsieur Nicolas, French Consul at Resht, published a very careful and very good edition of the text, from a lithograph copy at Teheran, comprising 464 Rubáiyát, with translation and notes of his own.

M. Nicolas, whose edition has reminded me of several things, and instructed me in others, does not consider Omar to be the material epicurean that I have literally taken him for, but a mystic, shadowing the Deity under the figure of wine, wine-bearer, etc., as Háfiz is supposed to do ; in short, a Súfi poet like Háfiz and the rest.

I cannot see reason to alter my opinion, formed as it was more than a dozen years ago [1] when Omar was first shown to me by one to whom I am indebted for all I know of Oriental, and very much of other, literature. He admired Omar's genius so much, that he would gladly have adopted any such interpretation of his meaning as M. Nicolas' if he could.[2] That he could not appears by his paper in the *Calcutta Review*, already so largely quoted, in which he argues from the poems themselves as well as from what records remain of the poet's life.

And if more were needed to disprove M. Nicolas' theory, there is the Biographical Notice which he himself has drawn up in direct contradiction

---

[1] Written in 1868.

[2] Perhaps would have edited the poems himself some years ago. He may now as little approve of my version on one side as of M. Nicolas' theory on the other.

of the poems given in his Notes (see pp. xiii, xiv of his Preface). Indeed, I hardly knew poor Omar was so far gone till his apologist informed me. For here we see that, whatever were the wine that Háfiz drank and sang, the veritable juice of the grape it was which Omar used, not only when carousing with his friends, but (says M. Nicolas) in order to excite himself to that pitch of devotion which others reached by cries and " hurlemens ". And yet, whenever wine, wine-bearer, etc., occur in the text—which is often enough—M. Nicolas carefully annotates " Dieu ", " La Divinité ", etc. : so carefully indeed that one is tempted to think that he was indoctrinated by the Súfi with whom he read the poems. (Note to Rub. 11, p. 8.) A Persian would naturally wish to vindicate a distinguished countryman : and a Súfi to enrol him in his own sect which already comprises all the chief poets in Persia.

What historical authority has M. Nicolas to show that Omar gave himself up " avec passion à l'étude de la philosophie des Soufis " ? (Preface, p. xiii.) The doctrines of Pantheism, Materialism, Necessity, etc., were not peculiar to the Súfi ; nor to Lucretius before them ; nor to Epicurus before him ; probably the very original Irreligion of thinking men from the first ; and very likely to be the spontaneous growth of a philosopher living in an age of social and political barbarism, under shadow of one of the two-and-seventy religions supposed to divide the world. Von Hammer (according to Sprenger's *Oriental Catalogue*) speaks of Omar as " a free-thinker, and *a great opponent of Súfism* " ; perhaps because, while holding much of their doctrine, he would not pretend to any inconsistent severity of morals. Sir W. Ouseley has written a note to something of the same effect on the fly-leaf of the Bodleian MS. And in two Rubáiyát of M. Nicolas' own edition Súf and Súfi are both disparagingly named.

No doubt many of these quatrains seem unaccountable unless mystically interpreted ; but many more as unaccountable unless literally. Were the wine spiritual, for instance, how wash the body with it when dead ? Why make cups of the dead clay to be filled with " La Divinité " by some succeeding mystic ? M. Nicolas himself is puzzled by some " bizarres " and " trop Orientales " allusions and images—" d'une sensualité quelquefois révoltante " indeed—which " les convenances " do not permit him to translate ; but still which the reader cannot but refer to " La Divinité ".[1] No doubt also many of the quatrains in the Teheran, as in the Calcutta, copies, are spurious ; such *Rubáiyát* being the common form of epigram in Persia. But this, at best, tells as much one way as

---

[1] A Note to quatrain 234 admits that, however clear the mystical meaning of such images must be to Europeans, they are not quoted without " rougissant " even by laymen in Persia—" Quant aux termes de tendresse qui commencent ce quatrain, comme tant d'autres dans ce recueil, nos lectures, habitués maintenant à l'étrangeté des expressions si souvent employées par Khéyam pour rendre ses pensées sur l'amour divin, et à la singularité de ses images trop Orientales, d'une sensualité quelquefois révoltante, n'auront pas de peine à se persuader qu'il s'agit de la Divinité, bien que cette conviction soit vivement discutée par les moullahs musulmans et même par beaucoup de laïques, qui rougissent véritablement d'une pareille licence de leur compatriote à l'egard des choses spirituelles."

another ; nay, the Súfi, who may be considered the scholar and man of letters in Persia, would be far more likely than the careless epicure to interpolate what favours his own view of the poet. I observe that very few of the more mystical quatrains are in the Bodleian MS., which must be one of the oldest, as dated at Shiráz A.H. 865, A.D. 1460. And this, I think, especially distinguishes Omar (I cannot help calling him by his—no, not Christian—familiar name) from all other Persian poets : that, whereas with them the poet is lost in his song, the man in allegory and abstraction ; we seem to have the man—the *bonhomme*—Omar himself, with all his humours and passions, as frankly before us as if we were really at table with him, after the wine had gone round.

I must say that I, for one, never wholly believed in the mysticism of Háfiz. It does not appear there was any danger in holding and singing Súfi Pantheism, so long as the poet made his salaam to Mohammed at the beginning and end of his song. Under such conditions Jeláluddín, Jámí, Attár and others sang ; using wine and beauty indeed as images to illustrate, not as a mask to hide, the Divinity they were celebrating. Perhaps some allegory less liable to mistake or abuse had been better among so imflammable a people : much more so when, as some think with Háfiz and Omar, the abstract is not only likened to, but identified with, the sensual image ; hazardous, if not to the devotee himself, yet to his weaker brethren ; and worse for the profane in proportion as the devotion of the initiated grew warmer. And all for what ? To be tantalized with images of sensual enjoyment which must be renounced if one would approximate a God, who according to the doctrine, *is* sensual matter as well as spirit, and into whose universe one expects unconsciously to merge after death, without hope of any posthumous beatitude in another world to compensate for all one's self-denial in this. Lucretius' blind divinity certainly merited and probably got as much self-sacrifice as this of the Súfi ; and the burden of Omar's song—if not " Let us eat "—is assuredly " Let us drink, for to-morrow we die ! " And if Háfiz meant quite otherwise by a similar language, he surely miscalculated when he devoted his life and genius to so equivocal a psalmody as from his day to this, has been said and sung by any rather than spiritual worshippers.

However, as there is some traditional presumption, and certainly the opinion of some learned men, in favour of Omar's being a Súfi—and even something of a saint—those who please may so interpret his wine and cup-bearer. On the other hand, as there is far more historical certainty of his being a philosopher, of scientific insight and ability far beyond that of the age and country he lived in ; of such moderate worldly ambition as becomes a philosopher, and such moderate wants as rarely satisfy a debauchee ; other readers may be content to believe with me that while the wine Omar celebrates is simply the juice of the grape, he bragged more than he drank of it, in very defiance perhaps of that spiritual wine which left its votaries sunk in hypocrisy and disgust.

Omar Khayyám	*Paraphrase*

Omar Khayyám

حورشید کند صبح بر بام افگند

کیخسرو روز باده در جام افگند

می خور که منادی‌ٔ سحرگه خیزان

آوازهٔ اشربوا در ایّام افگند

Paraphrase

(dome)

On lofty roof the sun has cast his rays,

The King of Day to fill his cup essays

     With wine; then quaff. The Muezzin of the dawn

"Drink Ye" has chanted forth "into the days".

آمد سحری ندا ز میخانهٔ ما

کای رند خراباتی دیوانهٔ ما

برخیز که پر کنیم پیمانه زمی

زان پیش که پر کنند پیمانهٔ ما

One morn from out our tavern came a cry :—

"Rise! Tavern-haunting madman. Time doth fly.

     Rise! Let us fill our measures with fresh wine

Ere Fate doth fill our measure 'neath the sky."

هنگام صبوح است وخروش ای ساقی

ماومی وکوی میفروشان ای ساقی

چه جای صلاحست خموش ای ساقی

بگذر ز حدیث زهد ونوش ای ساقی

Now for the early draught and first Cock-crow!

Hurrah for wine and wine-shops that we know!

     No time for good advice. O Saki. Hush!

Away with fasts! and let the wine-jug flow!

وقتی‌ست که از سبزه جهان آرایند

موسی صفتان ز شاخ کف بنمایند

عیسی نفسان ز خاک بیرون آیند

در چشم سحاب دیده‌ها بکشایند

(a)

The spring has come, the world in green is dight,

Like Moses buds put forth their hands to light,

     With Jesus' breath herbs from the ground arise

And flowers to weeping skies unveil their sight.

اکنون که جهان‌را بخوشی دست رسیست

هرزنده دلی را سوی صحرا هوسیست

بر هر شاخی طلوع موسی دستیست

در هر نفسی خروش عیسی نفسیست

(b)

The jocund spring doth now the world delight,

And hearts attuned yearn for the country bright.

     Each bough parades the sheen of Moses' hand

The breath of Christ is felt in zephyrs slight.

FitzGerald, 1st edition

I

Awake! for Morning in the Bowl of
   Night

Has flung the Stone that puts the Stars
   to Flight:

   And lo! The Hunter of the East has
   caught

The Sultán's Turret in a Noose of Light.

II

Dreaming when Dawn's Left Hand was
   in the Sky

I heard a Voice within the Tavern cry,
   "Awake, my little ones, and fill the
   cup,

Before Life's Liquor in its Cup be dry."

III

And as the Cock crew, those that stood
   before

The Tavern shouted "Open then the
   Door!

   You know how little while we have
   to stay,

And, once departed, may return no more."

IV

Now the New Year reviving old Desires,

The thoughtful Soul to Solitude retires,

   Where the WHITE HAND OF MOSES
   on the Bough

Puts out, and Jesus from the Ground
   suspires.

FitzGerald, 4th edition

I

Wake! For the Sun, who scatter'd into
   flight

The Stars before him from the Field of
   Night,

   Drives Night along with them from
   Heav'n and strikes

The Sultán's Turret with a Shaft of Light.

II

Before the phantom of False morning died
Methought a Voice within the Tavern
   cried,

   "When all the Temple is prepared
   within,

Why nods the drowsy Worshipper outside?"

III

The same as 1st edition.

IV

The same as 1st edition.

Omar Khayyám　　　　　　　　　　　　*Paraphrase*

No parallel.

روزیست خوش و هوانه گرم است نه سرد
ابر از رخ گلزار همی شوید گرد
بلبل بزبان حال با گل زرد
فریاد همی زند که می باید خورد

The air is temper'd and the day is fine,

A shower has wash'd the dust from herb and vine,
　The Nightingale to yellow rose complains
" We must drink wine. We must. We must drink wine."

هر روز برانم که کنم شب توبه
از جام و پیالهٔ لبالب توبه
اکنون که رسید وقت گل ترکمده
در موسم گل ز توبه یارب توبه

Each morn I promise penance for the night,

From cup and brimming goblet of delight;
　But now, when roses bloom, grant me release,
Now hold, O Lord, penance for penance right.

هنگام صبوح ای صنم فرخ پی
پرساز ترانه و پیش آوری
کافگند بخال صد هزاران جم و کی
این آمدن تیرماه و رفتن دی

Idol of happy feet! Bring forth, I pray,

The morning draught and on the viol play;
　For spring and winter by their lapse, in dust
Have many Jams, and Kais too, cast away.

چون می گذرد عمر چه شیرین و چه تلخ
پیمانه چو پرشود چه بغداد و چه بلخ
می نوش که بعد از من و تو ماه بسی
از سلخ بغرّه آید از غرّه بسلخ

In Baghdad or in Balkh need we complain

If our life passes well, or with some pain?

　Drink wine, for after us, our measure filled,
Full many moons shall wax and many wane.

FitzGerald, 1st edition

V

Irám indeed is gone with all its Rose,
And Jamshýd's Sev'n-ringed Cup, where
 no one knows ;
  But still the Vine her ancient Ruby
  yields,
And still a Garden by the Water blows.

VI

And David's Lips are lock't; but in
 divine
High piping Pehleví with "Wine!
 Wine! Wine!
  Red Wine!" the Nightingale cries to
  the Rose
That yellow Cheek of her's to incarnadine.

VII

Come, fill the Cup, and in the Fire of
 Spring
The Winter Garment of Repentance
 fling ;
  The Bird of Time has but a little way
To fly—and lo! the Bird is on the Wing.

VIII

And, look—a thousand Blossoms with the
 Day
Woke—and a thousand scattered into
 Clay ;
  And this first Summer Month that
  brings the Rose
Shall take Jamshýd and Kaikobád away.

FitzGerald, 4th edition

V

Iram indeed is gone with all his Rose,
And Jamshýd's Sev'n-ringed Cup, where
 no one knows ;
  But still a Ruby kindles in the Vine
And many a Garden by the Water blows.

VI

And David's lips are lockt; but in
 divine
High-piping Pehleví, with "Wine!
 Wine! Wine!
  Red Wine!" the Nightingale cries to
  the Rose
That sallow cheek of her's to incarnadine.

VII

Come, fill the Cup, and in the fire of
 Spring
Your Winter-garment of Repentance
 fling ;
  The Bird of Time has but a little way
To flutter—and the Bird is on the Wing.

VIII

Whether at Naishápúr or Babylon,
Whether the Cup with sweet or bitter
 run,
  The Wine of Life keeps oozing drop
  by drop
The Leaves of Life keep falling one by
 one.

Omar Khayyám	*Paraphrase*

از آمدن بهار و ز رفتن دی

اوراق وجود ما همیگردد طی

می خور مخوراندوه که گفتست حکیم

غمهای جهان چو زهرو تریاقش می

From warmth of Spring and Winter's biting cold

The leaves of Life are shrivelled, fold on fold.

    Drink wine and be not sad, a Sage has said

Grief kills like poison, wine as cure we hold.

تا در تن تست استخوان ورگ و پی

از خانهٔ تقدیر منه بیرون پی

گردن منه ار خصم بود رستم زال

منّت مکش ار دوست بود حاتم طی

While sinews serve thee well, bones, veins, and thigh,

Keep in the limits where thy Fate doth lie;

    Yield not thy neck if Rustum threaten thee,

Accept no favour from a Hátim Tai.

(a)

من هیچ ندانم که مرا آنکه سرشت

از اهل بهشت کرد یا دوزخ زشت

جامی و بتی و بربطی بر لب کشت

این هر سه مرا نقد ترا نسیهٔ بهشت

I know not if He who created me

Made me from hellish folk or heavenly;

    A cup, a Mistress singing by the tilth,

To me were joy—and heaven be to thee!

(b)

گر دست دهد ز مغز گندم نانی

وز می کد وئی ز گوسفندی رانی

با ماهرخی نشسته در ویرانی

عیشی بود آن نه حدّ هر سلطانی

If fortune favours me with bread of wheat,

A gourd of wine, sufficiency of meat,

    With beauty sitting by me in the wild,

Kings in my happiness may not compete.

گویند بهشت عدن با حور خوش است

می گویم که آب انگور خوش است

این نقد بگیر و دست از آن نسیه بدار

کاواز دهل برادر از دور خوش است

They tell of Paradise with Houris bright,

I say, for me the juice of grapes is right.

    Oh! take the cash and let the credit go!

The sound of drums far off cannot affright.

IX

Each Morn a thousand Roses brings,
  you say ;
Yes, but where leaves the Rose of
  Yesterday ?
  And this first Summer month that
    brings the Rose
Shall take Jamshýd and Kaikobád away.

IX

But come with old Khayyám and leave
  the Lot
Of Kaikobád and Kaikhosrú forgot :
  Let Rustum lay about him as he will,
Or Hatim Tai cry supper—heed them
  not.

X

Well, let it take them ! What have we
  to do
With Kaikobád the Great, or Kai-
  khosrú ?
  Let Zál and Rustum bluster as they
    will
Or Hátim call to Supper—heed not you.

X

With me along some strip of Herbage
  strown
That just divides the desert from the
  sown,
  Where name of Slave and Sultán
    scarce is known,
And pity Sultán Máhmúd on his Throne.

XI

With me along the strip of Herbage
  strown
That just divides the desert from the
  sown,
  Where name of Slave and Sultán is
    forgot—
And Peace to Máhmúd on his golden
  Throne.

XI

Here with a Loaf of Bread beneath the
  Bough,
A Flask of Wine, a Book of Verse—and
  Thou
  Beside me singing in the Wilderness—
And Wilderness is Paradise enow.

XII

A Book of Verses underneath the Bough,

A Jug of Wine, a Loaf of Bread—and
  Thou
  Beside me singing in the Wilderness—
Oh ! Wilderness were Paradise enow !

XII

" How sweet is mortal Sovrainty ! "—
  think some ;
Others " How blest the Paradise to
  come ! "
  Ah ! take the Cash in hand and waive
    the Rest ;
Oh, the brave Music of a *distant* Drum !

XIII

Some for the Glories of this World ;
  and some
Sigh for the Prophets Paradise to come ;

  Ah ! take the Cash and let the Credit
    go,
Nor heed the rumble of a distant Drum !

Omar Khayyám	*Paraphrase*
گل گفت که دست زر فشان آوردم	List to the rose : " My gold I scatter wide
خندان خندان سر بجهان آوردم	Laughing I blow upon the country-side,
بنداز سرکیسه برگرفتم رفتم	And as I go I loose my purse's string
هر نقد که بود در میان آوردم	And every coin to strangers I divide."

دنیا همه سربسر زر خواسته گیر	Assume that miser's gold the world o'erlay,
صد گنج بزر و گهر آراسته گیر	That hoards in hundred's jewelled wealth display,
پس بر سرآن گنج چو برصحرا برف	Then lo ! a day or two and all is spent,
روزی دو سه بنشسته و بر خاسته گیر	As on the desert snow that melts away.

زان پیش که بر سرت شبیخون آرند	Before men take thy life with murd'rous blow
فرمای که تا باده گلگون آرند	Bid wine be brought of clear and rosy glow,
تو زر نهٔ ای غافل نادان که ترا	Thou art not gold, O Fool, that careful men
درخاک نهند و باز بیرون آرند	Should bury deep and then raise from below.

این کهنه رباطرا که عالم نام است	This ancient Inn, the world, as I would say,
آرامگه ابلق صبح و شام است	Shelters the piebald horse of night and day.
بزمیست که وا ماندهٔ صد جمشید است	A feast it is by Jamshids left behind,
قصریست که تکیه گاهٔ صد بهرام است	A palace, too, where Bahráms pillow'd stay.

آن قصر که بهرام در و جام گرفت	Great Bahrám's palace where he drank with zest !
روبه بچه کرد و شیر آرام گرفت	In it the Fox has whelped and Lions rest ;
بهرام که گورمی گرفتی دائم	And Bahrám that kept hunting the wild ass,
امروز نگر که گور بهرام گرفت	To-day the grave has caught and quite supprest.

XIII

Look to the Rose that blows about us
    " Lo,
Laughing," she says, " into the World I
    blow
At once the silken Tassel of my Purse
Tear, and its Treasure on the Garden
    throw."

XIV

Look to the blowing Rose about us—" Lo,

Laughing," she says, " into the World I
    blow.
At once the silken tassel of my Purse
Tear, and its Treasure, on the Garden
    throw."

XIV

The Worldly Hope men set their Hearts
    upon
Turns Ashes—or it prospers ; and anon,

    Like Snow upon the Desert's dusty
      Face
Lighting a little Hour or two, is gone.

XV

And those who husbanded the Golden
    grain
And those who flung it to the Winds like
    Rain,
    Alike to no such aureate Earth are
      turn'd
As buried once, Men want dug up again.

XV

And those who husbanded the Golden
    Grain,
And those who flung it to the winds like
    Rain,
    Alike to no such aureate Earth are
      turn'd
As, buried once, Men want dug up again.

XVI

The Worldly Hope men set their Hearts
    upon
Turns Ashes, or it prospers ; and anon,

    Like Snow upon the Desert's dusty
      Face
Lighting a little hour or two—is gone.

XVI

Think, in this batter'd Caravanserai
Whose Doorways are alternate Night
    and Day
    How Sultán after Sultán with his
      Pomp
Abode his Hour or two, and went his
    way.

XVII

Think, in this batter'd Caravanserai
Whose Portals are alternate Night and
    Day,
    How Sultán after Sultán with his
      Pomp
Abode his destined Hour, and went his
    way.

XVII

They say the Lion and the Lizard keep
The Courts where Jamshýd gloried and
    drank deep ;
    And Bahrám that great Hunter, the
      Wild Ass
Stamps o'er his Head, and he lies fast
    asleep.

XVIII

They say the Lion and the Lizard keep
The Courts where Jamshýd gloried and
    drank deep ;
    And Bahrám that great Hunter, the
      Wild Ass,
Stamps o'er his Head, but cannot break
    his Sleep.

c

Omar Khayyám	*Paraphrase*
در هر دشتی که لاله زاری بودست	In every desert where a Tulip glows
آن لاله ز خون شهریاری بودست	This Bloom from blood of some dead Monarch blows,
هر برگ بنفشه کز زمین می روید	The Violet's leaf that springs from out the ground,
خالیست که بر رخ نگاری بودست	As mole from cheek of some dead beauty grows.

هر سبزه که در کنار جوی رستست	The verdure growing by the water-way
گوئی ز لب فرشته خوئی رستست	Springs from an Angel's lip, as Poets say.
هان بر سر سبزه پا بخواری ننهی	Tread gently then, for every flower that blows,
کان سبزه ز خاک لاله روئی رستست	Springs from the dust where some fair lady lay.

ای دوست بیا تا غم فردا نخوریم	Come friend! Despair not for to-morrow's fears
وین یکدم عمر را غنیمت شمریم	But pluck the golden fruit the present bears.
فردا که ازین دیر کهن درگذریم	To-morrow! when we leave this ancient house
با هفت هزار سالگان سر بسریم	We shall be one with seven thousand years.

یاران موافق همه از دست شدند	Old Friends are gone; and we remain while they
در پای اجل یگان یگان پست شدند	Fell at Death's feet. For Life, as guests so gay
بودند بیک شراب در مجلس عمر	Had bid us to his Court, and they, one round
دوری دو ز ما پیشترک مست شدند	Or two, before us drank—and went their way.

FitzGerald, 1st edition

XVIII

I sometimes think that never blows so red
The Rose as where some buried Cæsar
    bled ;
    That every Hyacinth the Garden
    wears
Dropt in its Lap from some once lovely
    Head.

XIX

And this delightful Herb whose tender
    Green
Fledges the River's lip on which we lean—
    Ah ! lean upon it lightly ! for who
    knows
From what once lovely lip it springs
    unseen !

XX

Ah ! My Belovéd, fill the cup that clears
To-DAY of past Regrets and future fears—

    To-morrow ? Why, To-morrow I may
    be
Myself with Yesterday's Sev'n Thousand
    Years.

XXI

Lo ! Some we loved, the loveliest and
    best
That Time and Fate of all their Vintage
    prest,
    Have drunk their Cup, a Round or two
    before,
And one by one crept silently to Rest.

FitzGerald, 4th edition

XIX

I sometimes think that never blows so red
The Rose as where some buried Cæsar
    bled ;
    That every Hyacinth the Garden
    wears
Dropt in her Lap from some once lovely
    Head.

XX

And this reviving Herb whose tender
    Green
Fledges the River-Lip on which we lean—
    Ah ! lean upon it lightly ! for who
    knows
From what once lovely lip it springs
    unseen.

XXI

Ah ! My Belovéd, fill the cup that clears
To-DAY of past Regrets and Future
    Fears :
    To-morrow ! Why, To-morrow I may
    be
Myself with Yesterday's Sev'n Thousand
    Years.

XXII

For some we loved, the loveliest and the
    best
That from his Vintage rolling Time
    hath prest,
    Have drunk their Cup a Round or
    two before,
And one by one crept silently to rest.

Omar Khayyám	*Paraphrase*

(a)

برخیز ومخور غم جهان گذران

بنشین و جهان بشادمانی گذران

در طبع جهان اگر فدائی بودی

نوبت بخود تو نیامدی از دگران

Arise and be not sad for days so few

That pass—But pass thy days with pleasure due;
  If the old order stood without a change
To thee from others nought would e'er accrue.

(b)

ابرآمد و باز بر سر سبزه گریست

بی باده ارغوان نمی باید زیست

این سبزه که امروز تماشاگه ماست

تا سبزهٔ خاک ما تماشاگه کیست

The weeping clouds again the verdure spray,

And we with purple wine our lives must stay;
  The verdure that delights our eyes to-day,
Whom shall it please—enriched from our own clay?

مگذار که غصّه در حصارت گیرد

واندوه محال روزگارت گیرد

می خور بکنار سبزه و آب روان

زان پیش که خاک در کنارت گیرد

Allow no grief to seize thee in its hold,

And let no vain regrets thy soul enfold;
  Drink wine where verdure grows beside a stream,
Ere earth doth hold thee to its bosom cold.

قومی متفکّر اند در مذهب ودین

جمعی متحیّر اند در شک ویقین

ناگاه منادئی برآید ز کمین

کای بیخبران راه نه آنست و نه این

Some folk immersed in faith and doctrine were

And some confused 'twixt doubt and truth appear.
  Now, as he lurks, the Muezzin startling cries:—
"Fools! The right road is neither here nor there!"

آنها که ز پیش رفته اند ای ساقی

در خاک غرور خفته اند ای ساقی

رو باده خور و حقیقت از من بشنو

بادست هرآنچه گفته اند ای ساقی

All those that travelled on this road before

Have sunk to sleep in pride for ever more;
  Drink wine, my friend, and hear the truth from me,
Their words were nought but wind that passes o'er.

XXII

And we, that now make merry in the
    Room
They left, and Summer dresses in new
    Bloom,
    Ourselves must we beneath the Couch
        of Earth
Descend—ourselves to make a Couch—for
    whom ?

XXIII

And we that now make merry in the
    Room
They left, and Summer dresses in new
    bloom,
    Ourselves must we beneath the Couch
        of Earth
Descend—ourselves to make a Couch
    —for whom ?

XXIII

Ah ! make the most of what we yet may
    spend
Before we too into the Dust descend ;
    Dust into Dust, and under Dust, to lie,
Sans Wine, sans Song, sans Singer, and
    —sans End !

XXIV

The same as 1st edition.

XXIV

Alike for those who for To-DAY prepare,
And those that after a To-MORROW stare,

    A Muezzin from the Tower of Dark-
        ness cries
" Fools ! Your Reward is neither Here
    nor There ! "

XXV

Alike for those who for To-DAY prepare
And those that after some To-MORROW
    stare,
    A Muezzin from the Tower of
        Darkness cries
" Fools ! Your reward is neither Here
    nor There."

XXV

Why, all the Saints and Sages who
    discuss'd
Of the Two Worlds so learnedly, are
    thrust
    Like foolish Prophets forth ; their
        words to scorn
Are scatter'd, and their Mouths are stopt
    with dust.

XXVI

Why, all the Saints and Sages who
    discuss'd
Of the Two Worlds so wisely—they are
    thrust
    Like foolish Prophets forth ; their
        Words to scorn
Are scatter'd, and their Mouths are
    stopt with Dust.

Omar Khayyám	*Paraphrase*
می خور که بزیر گل بسی خواهی خفت	Drink wine. For long thou'lt sleep within the tomb.
بی مونس وبی حریف وبی همدم وجفت	No friend, no wife shall share thy narrow room ;
زنهار بکس مگو تو این راز نهفت	Beware ! To none this mystery impart,
هر لالهٔ پژمرده نخواهد بشگفت	" The wither'd Tulip ne'er again shall bloom."

(a)

یکچند بکودکی باستاد شدیم	In youth some time we with a Master spent,
یکچند باستادیٔ خود شاد شدیم	And with our learning we were well content ;
پایان سخن شنو که مارا چه رسید	Ponder the end, the lesson that we learnt,
از خاک بر آمدیم و چون باد شدیم	" We came from dust, and as the wind we went."

(b)

بازی بودم پریده ام ز عالم راز	I came as Falcon from the secret sky
باتوکه رسم ز پست علوه بفراز	To fly with thee from lower depths on high,
اینجا چو نیافتم کس محرم راز	But finding none that could explain— by that
زان درکه در آمدم برون رفتم باز	Same door, by which I came—back I did fly.

(c)

کس مشکل اسرار ازلرا نکشاد	No one untied the everlasting knot,
کس یکقدم از نهاد بیرون نه نهاد	No one has stepped a pace beyond his lot ;
من می نگرم ز مبتدی تا اوستاد	From Acolyte to Master I must look,
عجزیست بدست هرکه از مادرزاد	Each mother's son is helpless quite —God wot.

آورد باصطرابم اوّل بوجود	Me first confusedly to birth He brought,
جز حیرتم از حیات چیزی نفزود	Save wonderment at life increaséd nought ;
رفتیم باکراه و ندانیم چه بود	In deep disgust we went. We do not know,
زین آمدن و بودن زین رفتن مقصود	From coming, being, going, what is sought.

FitzGerald, 1st edition

XXVI

Oh ! come with old Khayyám, and leave
    the wise
To talk ; one thing is certain, that Life
    flies ;
  One thing is certain, and the Rest
    is Lies ;
The Flower that once has blown for ever
    dies.

FitzGerald, 4th edition

(Parallel with LXIII below.)

XXVII

Myself when young did eagerly frequent
Doctor and Saint, and heard great
    Argument
  About it and about ; but evermore
Came out by the same Door as in I went.

XXVII

Myself when young did eagerly frequent
Doctor and Saint, and heard great
    Argument
  About it and about ; but evermore
Came out by the same Door where in
    I went.

XXVIII

With them the seed of Wisdom did I
    sow,
And with my own hand labour'd it to
    grow ;
  And this was all the Harvest that I
    reap'd—
" I came like Water, and like Wind I go."

XXVIII

With them the Seed of Wisdom did I
    sow
And with mine own hand wrought to
    make it grow ;
  And this was all the Harvest that I
    reaped—
" I came like Water, and like Wind I go."

XXIX

Into this Universe, and *why* not knowing
Nor *whence*, like Water willy-nilly
    flowing ;
  And out of it, as Wind along the
    Waste,
I know not *whither*, willy-nilly blowing.

XXIX

The same as in 1st edition.

Omar Khayyám	*Paraphrase*
چون امدنم بمن نبُد روز نخست	Unask'd of old they fixed my natal day,
وین رفتن بی مراد عزِ میست درست	My going too is fixed beyond gainsay.
برخیز و میان به بند ای ساقیِ چست	Arise! and gird thyself, my servitor,
کاندوه جهان بمی فروخواهم شست	For I with wine will wash all griefs away.

ازجرمِ حضیض خاک تا اوجِ زحل	From depth of Earth to Saturn's height I shot,
کردم همه مشکلاتِ گردون را حل	To Heaven's problems too an answer got;
بیرون جستم ز بند هر مکر و حیّل	From every artifice I leaped forth free,
هر سدّ کشاده شد مگر بندِ اجل	All knots untied, except of Death the Knot.

	(a)
اسرارِ ازل را تو دانی و نه من	We do not know what was of old decreed
وین حرفِ معّما نه تو خوانی و نه من	And this enigma we lack skill to read;
هست از پسِ پرده گفتگوئی من و تو	Behind the veil they speak of " me and thee "
چون پرده بر افتد نه تو مانی و نه من	But when it's drawn—no more of us indeed!

	(b)
کس را پسِ پردهٔ قضا راه نشد	No one has found a road behind the veil,
وز سرّ خدا هیچکس آگاه نشد	No one to read God's secrets did prevail:
هفتاد و دو سال فکر کردم شب و روز	For two and sev'nty years I pondered well,
معلوم نگشت و قصّه کوتاه نشد	No explication came, not short the tale.

No parallel.

FitzGerald, 1st edition

XXX

What, without asking, hither hurried
  whence ?
And, without asking, *whither* hurried
  hence !
Another and another cup to drown

The Memory of this Impertinence !

FitzGerald, 4th edition

XXX

What, without asking, hither hurried
  whence ?
And, without asking, *whither* hurried
  hence !
  Oh ! many a Cup of this forbidden
    wine,
Must drown the memory of that
  insolence !

XXXI

Up from Earth's Centre through the
  Seventh Gate
I rose, and on the Throne of Saturn
  sate,
  And many Knots unravel'd by the
    Road ;
But not the Knot of Human Death and
  Fate.

XXXI

Up from Earth's Centre through the
  Seventh Gate
I rose, and on the Throne of Saturn
  sate ;
  And many a Knot unravel'd by the
    Road ;
But not the Master-knot of Human
  Fate.

XXXII

There was a Door to which I found no
  Key :
There was a Veil past which I could
  not see :
  Some little Talk awhile of ME and
    THEE
There seem'd—and then no more of
  THEE and ME.

XXXII

There was a Door to which I found no
  Key :
There was the Veil through which I
  might not see :
  Some little talk awhile of ME and THEE

There was—and then no more of THEE
  and ME.

No parallel.

XXXIII

Earth could not answer ; nor the Seas that
  mourn
In flowing Purple, of their Lord forlorn ;
  Nor rolling Heaven, with all his Signs
    reveal'd
And hidden by the sleeve of Night and
  Morn.

Omar Khayyám	*Paraphrase*

No parallel.

لب برلب کوزه بردم از غایت آز

تازو طلبم واستهٔ عمر دراز

بامن بزبان حال می گفت این راز

عمری چو تو بوده ام دمی بامن ساز

With zest my lip to a Jug's lip I held,

By longing for some clue to life impell'd,

"Exactly such as thou I lived my life,

A moment bear with me," it gurgling spelled.

این کوزه چومن عاشق زاری بوده است

در بند سرزلف نگاری بوده است

این دسته که در گردن او می بینی

دستیست که در گردن یاری بوده است

This jug, like me, its time in sighs did waste,

Ensnar'd by ringlets that some beauty grac'd.

The handle that you see upon its neck,

Was once an arm that some sweetheart embraced.

دی کوزه گری بدیدم اندر بازار

برتازه گلی لکد همی زدبسیار

وان گل بزبان حال باویی گفت

من همچو تو بوده ام مرا نیکو دار

I chanc'd to watch a Potter yesterday,

Who struck with many blows the humid clay;

The clay in scarce-heard murmurs him besought

"I was as thou. Be gentle with me, pray!"

بر چهرهٔ گل شبنم نوروز خوش است

در صحن چمن روی دل افروز خوش است

از دی که گذشت هرچه گویی خوش نیست

خوش باش زدی مگو که امروز خوش است

On New Year's day the dew glints on the rose,

Across the lawn my Sweetheart's beauty glows.

Of yesterday the story is not sweet;

Then let it be. To-day most sweetly goes.

FitzGerald, 1st edition

XXXIII

Then to the rolling Heav'n itself I cried

Asking, "What Lamp had Destiny to
guide
  Her little Children stumbling in the
  Dark ?"
And "A blind Understanding!" Heav'n
replied.

XXXIV

Then to this earthen Bowl did I adjourn
My Lip the secret Well of Life to learn ;
  And Lip to Lip it murmur'd—"While
  you live
Drink !—for once dead you never shall
return."

XXXV

I think the Vessel that with fugitive
Articulation answer'd, once did live,
  And merry-make ; and the cold Lip
  I kissed,
How many kisses might it take—and
give.

XXXVI

For in the Market-place, one Dusk of
Day,
I watched the Potter thumping his wet
Clay :
  And with its all obliterated Tongue
It murmur'd—"Gently, Brother, gently,
pray !"

XXXVII

Ah ! fill the Cup : What boots it to
repeat
How Time is slipping underneath our
Feet :
  Unborn TO-MORROW, and dead
  YESTERDAY,
Why put about them if TO-DAY be sweet !

FitzGerald, 4th edition

XXIX

Then of the THEE IN ME who works
behind
The Veil, I lifted up my hands to find

  A Lamp amid the Darkness ; and I
  heard,
As from Without—THE ME WITHIN THEE
BLIND !

XXXV

Then to the lip of this poor earthen Urn
I lean'd, the Secret of my Life to learn :
  And Lip to Lip it murmur'd—"While
  you live
Drink !—for once dead, you never shall
return."

XXXVI

I think the Vessel, that with fugitive
Articulation answer'd, once did live,
  And drink ; and Ah ! the passive
  Lip I kissed,
How many kisses might it take—and
give !

XXXVII

For I remember stopping by the way

To watch a Potter thumping his wet
Clay :
  And with its all-obliterated Tongue
It murmur'd—"Gently, Brother, gently,
pray !"

No parallel.

Omar Khayyám	*Paraphrase*

(a)

در کارگهٔ کوزه گری کردم رای

در پائهٔ چرخ دیدم استاد بپای

می کرد سبو و کوزه را دسته و سر

از کلّهٔ پادشاه واز دست گدای

I pondered at a Potter's, where he
    wrought ;
The Master stood beside his wheel in
    thought,
    For top and handle of two pots of clay

A princes skull and beggar's hand he
    brought.

(b)

بر کوزه گری پریر کردم گذری

از خاک همی نمود هردم هنری

من دیدم اگر ندید هر بی بصری

خاک پدرم بر کف هر کوزه گری

I saw a famous Potter t'other day,

Each moment brought of skill a fresh
    display.
    Though men devoid of vision saw it
    not,
On every hand I saw my Father's clay.

هر جرعه که ساقیش بخاک افشاند

در دیدهٔ گرم آتش غم بنشاند

سبحان الله تو باده می پنداری

آبیکه زصد درد دلت برهاند

Each drop the Saki to the ground doth
    throw,
May quench the fire in hidden eyes
    below.
    Praise God ! Thou thinkest wine a
    water that
Can free the heart assailed by woe on woe.

چون لاله بنوروز قدح گیر بدست

بالاهرخی اگر ترا فرصت هست

می نوش بخرّمی که این چرخ کهن

ناگاه ترا چو خاک گرداند پست

On New Year's day like Tulips raise the
    Cup
With one of tulip-cheeks (if so, thou'lt
    sup).
    With merry cheer drink wine, for all
    at once
The Heav'n shall turn thee down—as
    earth ploughed up.

کم کن طمع از جهان و می زی خرسند

وز نیک و بد زمانه بگسل پیوند

می برکف و زلف دلبری گیر که زود

هم بگذرد ونماند این روزی چند

As one contented live and curb desire,

Let nothing over thee Command acquire.

    Take wine and play with beauty's
    locks for soon
Shall pass for aye thy scheme of life entire.

No parallel.

XXXVIII

And has not such a story from of Old
Down Man's successive generations roll'd
  Of such a clod of saturated Earth,
Cast by the Maker into Human mould ?

No parallel.

XXXIX

And not a drop that from our Cups we
    throw
For Earth to drink of, but may steal
    below,
  To quench the fire of Anguish in some
    eye,
There hidden—far beneath, and long ago.

No parallel.

XL

As then the Tulip for her morning sup
Of Heav'nly Vintage from the soil looks
    up,
  Do you devoutly do the like, till
    Heav'n
To Earth invert you—like an empty Cup.

No parallel.

XLI

Perplext no more with Human or
    Divine
To-morrow's tangle to the winds resign,
  And lose your fingers in the tresses of
The Cypress-slender Minister of Wine.

Omar Khayyám	Paraphrase

خیّام اگر باده پرستی خوش باش
با ماهرخی اگر نشستی خوش باش
چون عاقبت الامر فنا خواهی شد
انگار که نیستی چو هستی خوش باش

Khayyám ! If thou dost worship wine—rejoice !
If happiness in love is thine—rejoice !
Since at the last thou'lt perish—then this life
As non-existent hold—in fine—rejoice !

در دایرهٔ سپهر ناپیدا غور
جامیست که جمله را چشاند بدور
چون نوبت تو رسد تو هم آه مکن
می نوش بخوشدلی که دورست بجور

In heav'n that hides what we unlearnt must learn,
Exists a cup that we must drain in turn.
Drink with good heart and when thy time shall come,
Sigh not, nor shun the draught from hand so stern.

ای دل ز غبار جسم اگر پاک شوی
تو روح مجرّدی بر افلاک شوی
عرش است نشیمن تو شرمت بادا
کائی و مقیم خطهٔ خاک شوی

O soul ! From earthy taint when purified,
As spirit free, thou shalt toward heaven ride ;
Thy home the empyrean ! Shame on thee
Who dost in this clay tenement reside !

خیّام تنت بخیمهٔ ماند راست
جان سلطان است و منزلش دار بقاست
فرّاش اجل ز بهر دیگر منزل
از پا فکند خیمه که سلطان بر خاست

Khayyám ! Thy body stands just like a tent,
Thy soul as Sultan is toward Heaven bent ;
The Sultan rises—and the Chamberlain,
Grim Death, strikes down the empty tenement.

خیّام اگرچه خرگهٔ چرخ کبود
زد خیمه ودر بست در گفت و شنود
چون شکل حباب باده در جام وجود
ساقی ازل هزار خیّام نمود

Khayyám ! Although the blue pavilioned sky
Its tent hath pitched, and holds its peace. On high
The Eternal Saki pours untold Khayyáms
That seem like bubbles in the cup—and fly.

FitzGerald, 1st edition	*FitzGerald, 4th edition*
	XLII

And if the Wine you drink, the Lip you
  press,
End in what All begins and ends in—
  Yes ;
    Think then you are TO-DAY what
    YESTERDAY
You were—TO-MORROW you shall not
  be less.

Parallel with XLVII below.

XLIII

So when that Angel of the darker Drink
At last shall find you by the river-brink,
  And, offering his Cup, invite your Soul
Forth to your Lips to quaff—you shall
  not shrink.

Parallel with XLVIII below.

XLIV

[1] Oh, if my soul can fling his Dust aside,

Why, if the soul can fling the Dust
  aside,
And naked on the Air of Heaven ride,
  Were't not a Shame, were't not a
  Shame for him,
In this clay carcase crippled to abide ?

And naked on the Air of Heaven ride,
  Is't not a shame, is't not a shame for
  Him
So long in this Clay Suburb to abide !

XLV

[1] Or is *that* but a Tent, where rests anon

'Tis but a Tent where takes his one day's
  rest
A Sultán to the realm of Death addrest ;
  The Sultán rises—and the dark
  Ferrásh
Strikes, and prepares it for another
  Guest.

A Sultán to his kingdom passing on
  And which the swarthy Chamberlain
  shall strike
Then when the Sultán rises to be gone ?

XLVI

And fear not lest Existence closing your
Account, and mine, should know the
  like no more ;
  The Eternal Sákí from the Bowl has
  pour'd
Millions of Bubbles like us, and will
  pour.

No parallel.

---

[1] These quatrains did not form part of the 1st edition, but are found in FitzGerald's introduction to it. Until I obtained a reprint of this introduction (Sept. 1930) I was unaware that FitzGerald had translated the word " farrásh " as " chamberlain ", as I disliking foreign terms had felt bound to do.

OMAR KHAYYAM

Omar Khayyám

Paraphrase

(a)

در یاب که از روح جدا خواهی رفت
در پردهٔ اسرار خدا خواهی رفت
می خور که ندانی از کجا آمدهٔ
خوش باش ندانی که کجا خواهی رفت

Know! From thy soul thy body shall
  depart,
Behind God's mystic veil thou'lt live
  apart.
  Drink wine! Thou dost not know
    whence thou hast come.
Rejoice! Thou know'st not whither
  bound thou art.

(b)

ای بس که نباشیم و جهان خواهد بود
بی نام ز ما و بی‌نشان خواهد بود
زین پیش نبودیم و نبُد هیچ خلل
زین پس چو نباشیم همان خواهد بود

Oh! The long years the world shall keep
  its frame,
When we have gone, and left no sign or
  name!
  For ages we were not—and all was
    well,
And when we pass it will be just the same.

این قافلهٔ عمر عجب می گذرد
در یاب دمیک با طرب می گذرد
ساقی غم فردای حریفان چه خوری
پیش آر پیالهٔ که شب می گذرد

Life's caravan moves past in wondrous-
  wise
Then make the most of time—in merry
  guise;
  Why let the morrow sadden thee for
    friends
O Saki? Pass the Cup. The night soon
  dies!

(a)

از منزل کفر تابدین یکنفس است
وز عالم شک تابیقین یکنفس است
این یکنفس عزیزرا خوش می دار
کز حاصل عمر ما همین یکنفس است

A single breath divides the false and true,

And doubt it separates from sureness too;

  Then make the most of what the
    present yields,
The harvests of our life are ever scant
  and few.

(b)

دل گفت مرا علم لدنی هوس است
تعلیم کن اگر ترا دست رس است
گفتم که الف گفت دگر هیچ مگو
در خانه اگر کس است یک حرف بس است

My heart conveyed her strong desire to
  learn
How inspiration made the Prophets burn.

  I "Alif" said. "Enough," said she,
    "If ONE
Is in the house, one letter serves the
  turn."

FitzGerald, 1st edition   *FitzGerald, 4th edition*

XLVII

When you and I behind the Veil are
  past
Oh! but the long, long while the World
  shall last
  Which of our Coming and Departure
  heeds
As the Sea's self should heed a pebble
  cast.

No parallel.

XXXVIII

One Moment in Annihilation's Waste,
One Moment, of the Well of Life to
  taste—
  The Stars are setting and the Caravan

Starts for the Dawn of Nothing.—Oh,
  make haste!

XLVIII

A Moment's Halt—a momentary taste
Of BEING from the Well amid the
  Waste—
  And Lo!—the phantom Caravan
  has reach'd
The NOTHING it set out from.—Oh, make
  haste!

XLIX

Would you that spangle of Existence
  spend
About THE SECRET—quick about it,
  Friend!
  A Hair perhaps divides the False and
  True—
And upon what, prithee, may life depend?

No parallel.

L

A Hair perhaps divides the False and
  True;
Yes; and a single Alif were the clue—
  Could you but find it—to the Treasure-
  house,
And peradventure to THE MASTER too;

No parallel.

D

Omar Khayyám   *Paraphrase*

آن باده که قابل صورها است بذات

گاها حیوان میشود و گاه نبات

تا ظن نبری که نیست گردد هیأت

موصوف بذات است اگر نیست صفات

(a)

That mystic essence that in all inheres,

As herb or animal disguised appears,

   And never dies, away with such a thought!

A nature known, and yet unknown it wears.

می بر کف من نه که دلم در تاب است

وین عمر گریز پای چون سیماب است

برخیز که بیداری دولت خواب است

دریاب که آتش جوانی آب است

(b)

Stay me with wine, my heart with fervour glows,

And life as mercury unstable flows;

   Arise! For thy good fortune is a dream,

And · know, the fire of youth as water goes.

گه گشته نهان روی بکس ننمائی

گه در صور کون و مکان پیدائی

ای جلوه گری بخویشتن بنمائی

خود عین عیانی و خودی بینائی

At times Thou hid'st Thyself from human view,

Again art seen in worldly forms anew;

   Oh! Manifest Thy glory to Thyself,

Thou the Spectator art and thing seen too.

دل سرّ حیات ار کماهی دانست

در موت هم اسرار آلهی دانست

امروز که با خودی ندانستی هیچ

فردا که ز خود روی چه خواهی دانست

If now of life the secrets were revealed,

In death God's hidden things were not concealed;

   To-day you nothing know; To-morrow shall

To you, not you, the hidden doorway yield?

آنان که اسیر عقل و تمیز شدند

در حسرت هست و نیست ناچیز شدند

رو باخبرا توآب انگور گزین

کان بیخبران بغورهٔ مویز شدند

The hide-bound thralls of theory and thought

Have wrangled about Life, and come to nought.

   Go, prudent youth, let wine suffice. For these

Raw minds from unripe grapes have rawness caught.

FitzGerald, 1st edition   *FitzGerald, 4th edition*

LI
Whose secret Presence, through Creation's
 veins
Running Quicksilver-like eludes your
 pains ;
 Taking all shapes from Máh to Máhi ;
 and
They change and perish all, but He
 remains ;

No parallel.

LII
A moment guess'd, then back behind the
 Fold
Immerst of Darkness round the Drama
 roll'd
 Which, for the Pastime of Eternity,
He doth Himself contrive, enact, behold.

No parallel.

LIII
But if in vain, down on the stubborn floor
Of Earth, and up to Heav'ns unopening
 Door,
 You gaze TO-DAY, while You are You
 —how then
To-MORROW, You when shall be You no
 more ?

No parallel.

XXXIX
How long, how long, in infinite Pursuit

Of This and That endeavour and
 dispute ?
 Better be merry with the fruitful
 Grape
Than sadden after none, or bitter, Fruit.

LIV
Waste not your Hour, nor in the vain
 pursuit
Of This and That endeavour and dispute ;

 Better be jocund with the fruitful
 Grape
Than sadden after none, or bitter, Fruit.

Omar Khayyám   *Paraphrase*

من باده بجام یك منی خواهم کرد

خود را بدو جام می غنی خواهم کرد

اوّل سه طلاق عقل ودین خواهم داد

پس دختر رز را بزنی خواهم کرد

To-night I'll drink one cup for pleasure's sake,
Then with two cups myself I'll richer make ;
At first my faith and reason I'll divorce,

The vine's red daughter then to spouse I'll take.

من ظاهر نیستی وهستی دانم

من باطن هرفراز وپستی دانم

با این همه از دانش خود بیزارم

گرمرتبه ٔ ورای مستی دانم

"To be" and "not to be" I hardly know
But well acquainted am with "high" and "low" ;
And yet I weary of my own concept

If higher aught than wine I try to show.

دشمن بغلط گفت که من فلسفیم

ایزد داند که آنچه او گفت نیم

لیکن چو درین غم آشیان آمده ام

آخرکم ازان که من ندانم کیم

My foes misname me as "philosopher",

God knows I am not what they thus infer ;
But in this dark abode the case is worse,

For who I am—I can't at all aver.

سرمست به میخانه گذر کردم دوش

پیری دیدم مست وسبوئی بردوش

گفتم زخدا شرم نداری ای پیر

گفتاکرم از خداست رو باده نوش

In drink I passed a tavern yesterday

And saw a drunkard on whose shoulder lay
A great wine jar. "Art not ashamed," said I.
"Mercy's from God," quoth he, "Drink while you may."

می خور که ز توقلّت وکثرت به برد

واندیشه ٔ هفتاد ودو ملّت به برد

پرهیز مکن ز کیمیائی که ازو

یك جرعه ٔ هزار علّت به برد

Drink wine, for it will rectify excess,

And solve the riddle of the sects no less.

Refrain not from this subtle alchemy,

One draught a thousand reasons will redress.

XL

You know, my Friends, how long since
in my House
For a new Marriage I did make Carouse :
  Divorced old barren Reason from my
  Bed,
And took the Daughter of the Vine to
  spouse.

LV

You know, my Friends, with what a
brave Carouse
I made a Second Marriage in my house ;
  Divorced old barren Reason from my
  Bed,
And took the Daughter of the Vine to
  spouse.

XLI

For " is " and " is-not " though *with*
Rule and Line,
And " up-and-down " *without* I could
  define,
  I yet in all I only cared to know,
Was never deep in anything—but Wine.

LVI

For " is " and " is-not " though with
Rule and Line
And " up-and-down " by Logic I define,

  Of all that one should care to fathom, I
Was never deep in anything but—Wine.

LVII

Ah, but my Computations, People say,
Reduced the Year to better reckoning ?
    —Nay,
  'Twas only striking from the Calendar
Unborn To-morrow, and dead Yester-
  day.

No parallel.

XLII

And lately, by the Tavern Door agape,
Came stealing through the Dusk an Angel
  shape
  Bearing a Vessel on his Shoulder ; and
He bid me taste of it ; and 'twas—the
  Grape !

LVIII

And lately, by the Tavern Door agape
Came shining through the Dusk an Angel
  Shape
  Bearing a Vessel on his Shoulder ; and
He bid me taste of it ; and 'twas—the
  Grape !

XLIII

The Grape that can with Logic absolute
The Two-and-seventy jarring sects
  confute ;
  The subtle Alchemist that in a Trice
Life's leaden Metal into Gold transmute.

LIX

The Grape that can with Logic absolute
The Two-and-seventy jarring sects
  confute ;
  The sovereign Alchemist that in a trice
Life's leaden metal into Gold transmute :

Omar Khayyám   *Paraphrase*

No parallel.

می می خورم وهرکه چو من اهل بود

می خوردن من نزد او سهل بود

می خوردن من حق بازل می دانست

گر می نخورم علم خدا جهل بود

With worthy men in wine I take delight,

And drinking wine is harmless in their sight;
     For God foreknew of old this very thing,

If I abstain his knowledge was not right.

گویند مخور می که بلاکش باشی

در روز مکافات در آتش باشی

این هست ولی ز هردو عالم خوشتر

این یك دم کز شراب سرخوش باشی

" Abstain from wine," they say, " 'twill bring distress,

In hell at last they'll fling thee merciless."

     'Tis so. But sweeter than both worlds thou'lt find

The moment that from wine springs happiness.

See against XXVI (1st edition).   See paraphrase above.

بسیار بگشتیم بگرد درو دشت

اندر همه آفاق بگشتیم بگشت

از کس نشنیدیم که آمد زان راه

راهی که برفت راه روباز نگشت

Far wandered we past gates, or thro' the plain,

Through all the world our vagrant path has lain,

     Nor heard from one who has retraced the road,

That travelled once, no one may pass again.

XLIV

The mighty Mahmúd, the victorious
  Lord,
That all the misbelieving and black
  Horde
    Of Fears and Sorrows that infest the
    Soul
Scatters and slays with his enchanted
  Sword.

LX

The mighty Mahmúd, Allah-breathing
  Lord,
That all the misbelieving and black
  Horde
    Of Fears and Sorrows that infest the
    Soul
Scatters before him with his whirlwind
  Sword.

No parallel.

LXI

Why, be this Juice the growth of God,
  who dare
Blaspheme the twisted tendril as a
    Snare ?
    A Blessing, we should use it, should
    we not ?
And if a Curse—why, then, Who set it
  there ?

No parallel.

LXII

I must abjure the Balm of Life, I must
Scared by some After-reckoning ta'en on
    trust,
    Or lured with hope of some Diviner
    Drink,
To fill the Cup—when crumbled into
  Dust !

See XXVI above.

LXIII

Oh Threats of Hell and Hopes of
    Paradise !
One thing at least is certain.—*This* Life
  flies ;
    One thing is certain and the rest is
    Lies ;
The Flower that once has blown for ever
  dies.

No parallel.

LXIV

Strange is it not ? that of the myriads who
Before us pass'd the door of Darkness
    through,
    Not one returns to tell us of the Road
Which to discover we must travel too.

Omar Khayyám	Paraphrase

آنان که محیط فضل وآداب شدند
از جمع کمال شمع اصحاب شدند
ره زین شب تاریک نبردند برون
گفتند فسانه ٔ ودر خواب شدند

Learning and letters they that grasped, adept,
As candles bright the way for others kept.

No road they found thro' this dark night of gloom,
They told a tale and then in dust they slept.

بر ترز سپهر خاطرم روز نخست
لوح و قلم و بهشت ودوزخ می جست
پس گفت مرا معلّم از رای درست
لوح و قلم و بهشت ودوزخ باتشت

When first creation dawned beyond this sphere,
Of Heav'n and Hell, I sought some meaning clear;
    Then the Preceptor spoke: "The Tablet, Pen,
And Heav'n and Hell in thine own self inhere."

گردون کمری ز عمر فرسوده ٔ ماست
جیحون اثری ز اشک پالوده ٔ ماست
دوزخ شرری ز رنج بیهوده ٔ ماست
فردوس دمی ز وقت آسوده ٔ ماست

The sky's a girdle from life's rubbish swept,
Jihun's a mark of the pure tears we wept,
    Hell's but a spark from clash of worries struck,
Heav'n but a moment's rest midst turmoil kept.

بشنو ز من ای زبده ٔ یاران کهن
اندیشه مکن زین فلک بی سروبن
بر گوشه ٔ عرصه ٔ قیامت بنشین
بازیچه ٔ چرخ را تماشا میکن

Friends of my youth. A word take from my pen,
Heed not the heaven's senseless might. And then
    Apart from crowds contented stay and mark
The little game that heaven plays with men.

این چرخ فلک که ما در و حیرانیم
فانوس خیال ازو مثالی دانیم
خورشید چراغ دان و عالم فانوس
ما چون صوریم کاندر و حیرانیم

This wheeling sphere, that we with wonder know,
Resembles most a magic-lantern show;
    The sun as lamp, the world as lantern turns,
And we, bewildered figures, come and go.

FitzGerald, 1st edition   *FitzGerald, 4th edition*

                                                   LXV
                                                   The Revelations of Devout and Learn'd
                                                   Who rose before us, and as Prophets
                                                       burn'd,
No parallel.   Are all but Stories, which awoke from
                                                           sleep
                                                   They told their comrades, and to Sleep
                                                       return'd.

                                                   LXVI
                                                   I sent my soul through the Invisible,
                                                   Some letter of that After-life to spell:
No parallel.   And by and by my Soul return'd
                                                           to me,
                                                   And answer'd " I myself am Heav'n
                                                       and Hell ".

                                                   LXVII
                                                   Heav'n but the Vision of fulfill'd Desire,
                                                   And Hell the Shadow from a Soul on
No parallel.   fire,
                                                       Cast on the Darkness into which Our-
                                                           selves,
                                                   So late emerged from, shall so soon
                                                       expire.

            XLV
But leave the Wise to wrangle, and with me
The Quarrel of the Universe let be;
    And, in some corner of the Hubbub   No parallel.
        coucht,
Make game of that which makes as much
    of Thee.

            XLVI   LXVIII
For in and out, above, about, below,   We are no other than a moving row
'Tis nothing but a Magic Shadow-show,   Of Magic Shadow-shapes that come and
                                                       go
    Play'd in a Box whose Candle is the   Round with the Sun-illumined Lantern
        Sun,   held
Round which we Phantom Figures come   In Midnight by the Master of the Show;
    and go.

Omar Khayyám   *Paraphrase*

See against XLII, 4th edition.   See paraphrase above.

See against XLIII, 4th edition.   See paraphrase above.

از روی حقیقتی نه از روی مجاز

ما لعبتگانیم و فلک لعبت باز

بازیچه همی کنیم بر نطع وجود

رفتیم بصندوق عدم یکیک باز

We are but chess-men in a game of chess

Played by great heaven in its wayward-
ness,
Hither and thither on the board we
move,
And singly reach the box of nothingness.

ای رفته بچوگان قضا همچو گو

چپ می خور و راست میرو هیچ مگو

کانکس که ترا فگند اندر تل وپو

او داندو او داندو او داندو او

Thou, fallen like a ball to Fortune's
blows !
Speed left and right, in silence, as it
goes ;
For He that threw thee down into the
rush
He knows about it, and He knows. He
knows.

برلوح نشان بود پنهان بودست

پیوسته قلم ز نیک و بد آسودست

اندر تقدیر آنچه بایست بداد

غم خوردن و کوشیدن ما بیهودست

The tablet bears a secret impress writ ;

Of good or bad, the pen recks not one
whit ;
Whatever under Fate seemed right was
giv'n ;
'Tis vain to struggle and to fight with it.

FitzGerald, 1st edition

XLVII

And if the Wine you drink, the Lip you
  press,
End in the Nothing all Things end in.—
  Yes.—
  Then fancy while Thou art, Thou art
    but what
Thou shalt be—Nothing.—Thou shalt
  not be less.

XLVIII

While the Rose blows along the River
  Brink,
With old Khayyám the Ruby Vintage
  drink :
  And when the Angel with its darker
    Draught
Draws up to Thee—take that, and do not
  shrink.

XLIX

'Tis all a Chequer-board of Nights and
  Days
Where Destiny with Men for Pieces
  plays :
  Hither and thither moves, and mates,
    and slays,
And one by one back in the Closet lays.

L

The Ball no question makes of Ayes and
  Noes,
But Right or Left as strikes the Player
  goes ;
  And He that toss'd Thee down into
    the Field,
He knows about it all.—HE knows.—HE
  knows !

LI

The Moving Finger writes ; and having
  writ,
Moves on : nor all thy Piety nor Wit
  Shall lure it back to cancel half a Line,

Nor all thy Tears wash out a Word of it.

FitzGerald, 4th edition

See XLII above.

See XLIII above.

LXIX

But helpless Pieces of the Game He
  plays
Upon this Chequer-board of Nights and
  Days ;
  Hither and thither moves, and checks,
    and slays,
And one by one back in the Closet lays.

LXX

The Ball no question makes of Ayes and
  Noes,
But Here or There as strikes the Player
  goes ;
  And He that toss'd you down into
    the Field,
He knows about it all.—HE knows.—HE
  knows !

LXXI

The Moving Finger writes ; and having
  writ,
Moves on ; nor all your Piety nor Wit
  Shall lure it back to cancel half a
    Line ;
Nor all your Tears wash out a Word of it.

Omar Khayyám

Paraphrase

(a)

این چرخ چو طاسیست نگون افتاده

در او همه زیرکان زبون افتاده

در دوستی شیشه و ساغر نگرید

لب بر لب و درمیانه خون افتاده

Like an inverted cup the sky doth show,

Within it pent philosophers lie low;

  Observe the bond that holds the flask and cup,

With lip to lip between them blood doth flow.

(b)

نیکی و بدی که در نهاد بشر است

شادی و غمی که در قضا و قدرت است

با چرخ مکن حواله کاندر راه عقل

چرخ از تو هزار بار بیچاره تر است

The good and bad in thine own nature lie,

But fate decrees if you shall laugh or sigh;

  To Heav'n impute it not. In reason's path

It far more helpless is than you or I.

(a)

ای دل چو حقیقت جهان هست مجاز

چندین چه بری خواری از این رنج دراز

تن را بقضا سپار و با درد بساز

کین رفته قلم ز بهر تو نیاید باز

Dear heart! since truth itself is but pretence,

Why overborne by sorrow? Why and whence?

  Confide in Fate. Fret not. The pen moves on,

Nor will come back, for all thy vehemence.

(b)

See also against LI, 1st edition, and LXXI, 4th edition.

(a)

خوش باش که پخته اند سودای تو دی

ایمن شده از همه تمنّای تو دی

تو شاد بزی که بی تقضای تو دی

دادند قرار کار فردای تو دی

Lo! Yesterday they fixed to-day's career,

When all from thy deep longings was secure;

  Be well content! Unmoved by thee they fixed,

What thou must do to-morrow—and must bear.

(b)

As to the 3rd and 4th lines of LXXIV, 4th edition, see against XLVII, 4th edition, the last two lines of (a).

FitzGerald, 1st edition   *FitzGerald, 4th edition*

LII

And that inverted Bowl we call the Sky
Whereunder crawling coop't we live
    and die,
Lift not thy hands to *It* for help—for It

Rolls impotently on as Thou or I.

LXXII

And that inverted Bowl they call the sky,
Whereunder crawling coop't we live
    and die,
  Lift not your hands to *It* for help, for
    It
As impotently moves as you or I.

LIII

With Earth's first Clay They did the
    Last man's knead,
And then of the Last Harvest sow'd the
    Seed :
  Yea, the first Morning of Creation
    wrote
What the Last Dawn of Reckoning shall
    read.

LXXIII

With Earth's first clay they did the
    Last Man knead,
And there of the Last Harvest sow'd
    the Seed ;
  And the first Morning of Creation
    wrote
What the Last Dawn of Reckoning shall
    read.

LXXIV

YESTERDAY *This* Day's Madness did
    prepare ;
TO-MORROW's Silence, Triumph, or
    Despair :
  Drink ! for you know not whence you
    came nor why ;
  Drink ! for you know not why you go,
    nor where.

No parallel.

Omar Khayyám	*Paraphrase*
آن روز که توسن فلک زین کردند	When first they saddled horses of the sky,
آرایش مشتری و پروین کردند	When Jupiter, the Pleiads too, on high
این بود نصیب ما ز دیوان قضا	In splendour blazed—this was our lot from Fate ;
ما را چه گنه قسمت ما این کردند	For sin predestined how shall we reply ?
چون خود ازل بود مرا انشا کرد	In love eternal He created me
بر من ز نخست درس عشق املا کرد	And first He taught the lore of charity.
وانگاه قراضهٔ ریزهٔ قلب مرا	Then from my heart He filed a key that might
مفتاح خزاین در معنی کرد	Unlock the treasures of Reality.
با تو بخرابات اگر گویم راز	In some low Inn I'd rather seek Thy face,
به ز آنکه بمحراب کنم بی تو نماز	Than pray without Thee toward the Niche's place.
ای اوّل وای آخر خلقان همه تو	O First and Last of all ! As Thou dost will,
خواهی تو مرا بسوز و خواهی بنواز	Burn me in Hell—or save me by Thy grace !
	(*a*)
یزدان چو گل وجود ما می آراست	When God of our existence mixed the clay,
دانست ز فعل ما چه خواهد برخاست	He knew full well what works we should display.
بی حکمش نیست هر گناهی که مراست	No fault have I save by His own decree,
پس سوختن قیامت از بهرچه خواست	Then why should He burn me at judgment day ?
	(*b*)
حکمی که از او محال باشد پرهیز	Thy strict behest we cannot but fulfil
فرموده وامر کرده کز وی بگریز	And yet Thou say'st " Flee from it—I so will "
آنگاه میان امرو نهیش عاجز	Between Thy " Yea " and " Nay " we worldlings fail
در مانده جهانیان که کج دارو مریز	To slant the cup and yet no liquor spill.

LIV
I tell Thee this.—When starting from
   the Goal,
Over the shoulders of the flaming Foal
   Of Heav'n Parwin and Mushtara they
   flung,
In my predestined Plot of Dust and Soul

LXXV
I tell you this.—When started from the
   Goal,
Over the flaming shoulders of the Foal
   Of Heav'n Parwin and Mushtari they
   flung,
In my predestined Plot of Dust and Soul

LV
The Vine had struck a fibre; which
   about
If clings my Being—let the Súfi flout;

   Of my Base Metal may be filed a Key,
That shall unlock the Door he howls
   without.

LXXVI
The Vine had struck a fibre : which
   about
If clings my Being—let the Dervish
   flout;
   Of my Base metal may be filed a Key
That shall unlock the Door he howls
   without.

LVI
And this I know ; whether the one True
   Light
Kindle to Love, or Wrath consume me
   quite,
   One glimpse of It within the Tavern
   caught
Better than in the Temple lost outright.

LXXVII
And this I know ; whether the one True
   Light
Kindle to Love, or Wrath-consume me
   quite,
   One Flash of It within the Tavern
   caught
Better than in the Temple lost outright.

No parallel.

LXXVIII
What ! out of senseless Nothing to provoke
A conscious Something to resent the yoke
   Of unpermitted Pleasure, under pain
Of Everlasting Penalties, if broke !

Omar Khayyám

تا خاک مرا بقالب آميخته اند
پس فتنه که از خاک بر انگيخته اند
من بهتر ازين نمى توانم بودن
کز بوته مرا چنين برون ريخته اند

بر رهگذرم هزار جا دام نهى
گوئى که بگيرمت اگر گام نهى
يک ذرّه ز حکم تو جهان خالى نيست
حکم تو کنى و عاصيم نام نهى

من بندهٔ عاصى رضاى تو کجاست
تاريک دلم نور وصفاى تو کجاست
مرا تو بهشت اگر بطاعت بدهى
اين مزد بود لطف و عطاى تو کجاست

اى واقف اسرار ضمير همه کس
در حالت عجز دستگير همه کس
يارب تو مرا توبه ده و عذر پذير
اى توبه ده و عذر پذير همه کس

سازندهٔ کار مرده و زنده توئى
دارندهٔ اين چرخ پراگنده توئى
من گرچه بدم صاحب اين بنده توئى
کس را چه گنه که آفريننده توئى

Paraphrase

While for the mould they mixed my native clay
They caused in me the surge that I display.
Better than this I cannot be. For thus
They poured me from the crucible that day.

About my path Thou sett'st a thousand snares
And say'st "I'll catch thy footsteps unawares".
In everything Thy order rules the world,
Yet me, Thy creature, "rebel" it declares.

(a)
What pleasure hast Thou in a slave so base,
Whose darkened heart obscures Thy shining face;
If for Thy worship heaven is the meed,
'Tis naught but wages. Where Thy gift and grace?

(b)
Thou who dost know the secrets of each heart,
Thou who the Helper of the helpless art,
O Lord! Repentance give and take. For Thou
To all the grace of pardon dost impart.

(c)
The quick and dead are in Thy wide domain,
Thou dost uphold the heav'n, unstable, vain;
If I transgress, nathless Thy slave am I
And Thou my Maker art—who shall arraign?

*   *   *

FitzGerald, 1st edition

FitzGerald, 4th edition

LXXIX

What! from his helpless Creature be
   repaid
Pure Gold for what he lent him dross-
   allay'd
Sue for a Debt he never did contract,
And cannot answer. Oh! the sorry
   trade!

No parallel.

LVII

Oh Thou, who didst with Pitfall and
   with Gin
Beset the Road I was to wander in,
  Thou wilt not with Predestination
  round
Enmesh me, and impute my Fall to Sin?

LXXX

Oh Thou, who didst with pitfall and
   with gin,
Beset the Road I was to wander in,
  Thou wilt not with Predestined Evil
  round
Enmesh, and then impute my Fall to Sin!

LVIII

Oh, Thou, who Man of baser Earth
   didst make,
And who with Eden didst devise the
   snake;
  For all the Sin wherewith the Face of
  Man
Is blacken'd—Man's Forgiveness give—
   and take!
     *   *   *

LXXXI

Oh, Thou, who Man of baser Earth
   didst make,
And ev'n with Paradise devise the snake;

  For all the Sin wherewith the Face of
  Man
Is blacken'd—Man's forgiveness give—
   and take!
     *   *   *

E

Omar Khayyám   *Paraphrase*

KUZA

در کارگهٔ کوزه‌گری بودم دوش
دیدم دو هزار کوزه گویا و خموش
هر یك بزبان حال با من گفتند
کو کوزه‌گر و کوزه‌خرو کوزه‌فروش

I tarried at a potter's yesterday,

Two thousand pots speaking or silent lay :

  In their pot-language all began to say

" Where's the pot-maker, -buyer, -seller, pray ? "

جامیست که عقل آفرین می زندش
صد بوسه زمهر برجبین می زندش
این کوزه‌گر دهر چنین جام لطیف
میسازد و باز بر زمین می زندش

A cup there is that wisdom lauds enow,

And for its beauty kisses on its brow.

  So rare a cup the World's Great Potter makes,

And shatters on the ground again, I trow.

اجزای پیالهٔ که درهم پیوست
بشکستن آن روا نمی دارد دست
چندین سر و دست نازنین از سر دست
از مهر که پیوست و بکین که شکست

He who the pieces of a cup combined,

The same to shatter them had ne'er designed ;

  Such subtle handiwork, could He thro' love

That perfect made—destroy thro' malice blind ?

دارنده چو ترکیب طبائع آراست
باز از چه سبب فکندش اندر کم و کاست
گر نیك آمد شکستن از بهر چه بود
ور نیك نیامد این صور عیب کراست

When from God's hand our human natures came

Why thrust He them to needless loss and shame ?

  If they were good—why shatter them at all ?

If bad—for failure who must take the blame ?

FitzGerald, 1st edition   *FitzGerald, 4th edition*

NAMA

LIX

Listen again. One evening at the Close
Of Ramazán, ere the better Moon
   arose,
  In that old Potter's Shop I stood
   alone
With the clay Population round in Rows.

LXXXII

As under cover of departing Day
Slunk hunger-stricken Ramazán away,

  Once more within the Potter's house
   alone
I stood, surrounded by the Shapes of Clay.

LX

And strange to tell among that Earthen
   Lot
Some could articulate, while others not:

  And suddenly one more impatient
   cried,
" Who *is* the Potter, pray, and who the
   Pot ? "

LXXXIII

Shapes of all Sorts and Sizes, great and
   small,
That stood along the floor and by the
   wall ;
  And some loquacious Vessels were ;
   and some
Listen'd perhaps, but never talked at all.

LXI

Then said another—" Surely not in vain

My substance from the common Earth
   was ta'en,
  That He who subtly wrought me
   into Shape
Should stamp me back to common Earth
   again."

LXXXIV

Said one among them—" Surely not in
   vain
My substance of the common Earth was
   ta'en
  And to this Figure moulded, to be broke,

Or trampled back to shapeless Earth
   again."

LXII

Another said—" Why ne'er a peevish Boy,

Would break the Bowl from which he
   drank in Joy ;
  Shall He that *made* the Vessel in pure
   Love
And Fancy, in an after Rage destroy ! "

LXXXV

Then said a Second—" Ne'er a peevish
   Boy
Would break the Bowl from which he
   drank in joy ;
  And He that with his hand the Vessel
   made
Will surely not in after Wrath destroy."

LXIII

None answered this ; but after Silence
   spake
A vessel of a more ungainly Make :
  " They sneer at me for leaning all
   awry ;
What !   did the hand then of the Potter
   shake ? "

LXXXVI

After a momentary silence spake

Some vessel of a more ungainly Make ;
  " They sneer at me for leaning all
   awry :
What ! did the Hand then of the Potter
   shake ? "

Omar Khayyám · *Paraphrase*

See against LX, 1st edition. · See paraphrase above.

See paraphrase above.

گویند بحشر جستجو خواهد بود
وآن یار عزیز تندخو خواهد بود
از خیر محض جز نکوئی نیاید هرگز
خوش باش که عاقبت نکو خواهد بود

They say a search shall darkness all dispel
In that last day. The "Friend", too, shall repel.
　But from "The Perfect Good" no ill can come.
Be of good cheer. The end shall all be well.

در پای اجل چو من پراگنده شوم
وز بیخ امید عمر برکنده شوم
زنهار گلم بجز صراحی مکنید
باشد که ز باده پرشود زنده شوم

When Death has placed his foot on me amain,
And every hope of life from me is ta'en,
　A wine-jug you shall make of me; perhaps
With wine if filled, I yet may live again.

ماه رمضان برفت و شوّال آمد
هنگام نشاط عیش و قوّال آمد
آمد که آنکه خیکها اندر دوش
گویند که پشت پشت حمّال آمد

Ram'zán has gone, Shawwál is at the door,
Fresh joys shall gladden us and tales of yore.
　The porters stride with heavy loads of flasks
And cry—"Give way. The Porter comes once more."

FitzGerald, 1st edition

FitzGerald, 4th edition

LXXXVII
Whereat some of the loquacious Lot—
I think a Súfi pipkin—waxing hot.—
  "All this of Pot and Potter.—Tell
    me then,
Who is the Potter, pray, and who the
    Pot ? "

See LX above.

LXIV
Said one—" Folks of a surly Tapster tell,

And daub his Visage with the Smoke
  of Hell ;
  They talk of some strict testing of us.—
  Pish !
He's a Good Fellow, and 'twill all be
  well."

LXXXVIII
" Why," said another, " Some there are
    who tell
Of one who threatens he will toss to
    Hell
  The luckless Pots he marr'd in
    making.—Pish !
He's a Good Fellow, and 'twill all be
  well."

LXV
Then said another with a long-drawn
  Sigh,
" My Clay with long oblivion is gone dry :
  But, fill me with the old familiar
  juice,
Methinks I might recover by-and-bye ! "

LXXXIX
" Well," murmured one, " Let whoso
    make or buy,
My Clay with long Oblivion is gone dry ;
  But fill me with the old familiar Juice,

Methinks I might recover by and by."

LXVI
So while the Vessels one by one were
  speaking,
One spied the little Crescent all were
  seeking :
  And then they jogg'd each other,
  " Brother, Brother !
Hark to the Porter's Shoulder-knot a-
  creaking ! "
  *   *   *

XC
So while the Vessels one by one were
  speaking,
The little Moon look'd in that all were
  seeking :
  And then they jogg'd each other,
  " Brother, Brother !
Now for the Porter's shoulder-knot
  a-creaking ! "
  *   *   *

Omar Khayyám   *Paraphrase*

(a)

چون فوت شوم بباده شوئید مرا

تلقین ز شراب ناب گوئید مرا

خواهید که بروز حشر بینید مرا

از خاک در میکده جوئید مرا

Bathe me in wine, when I have passed away,

With purest wine the burial service say;

If you would see me in the day of doom

Seek me in dust beside the Inn's doorway.

(b)

زنهار مرا زجام می قوت کنید

وین چهرهٔ کهربا چو یاقوت کنید

چون در گذرم بمی بشوئید مرا

وز چوب رزم تختهٔ تابوت کنید

Take heed, my friends, and stay my heart with wine,

And make these amber cheeks like rubies shine;

And when I pass bathe me in wine— and make

My coffin from the wood of an old vine.

چندان بخورم شراب کین بوی شراب

آید ز تراب چون شوم زیر تراب

تا بر سر خاک من رسد مخموری

از بوی تراب من شود مست و خراب

My thirst in wine I'll quench with such intent

My very dust of wine shall waft the scent;

And Topers passing by their sense shall lose

Bemused by fragrance from such tenement.

طبعم به نماز و روزه چون مائل شد

گفتم که نجات کلّیم حاصل شد

افسوس که آن وضو ببادی بشکست

وآن روزه به نیم جرعهٔ می باطل شد

To prayer and fast my spirit did incline,

Salvation full and sure I thought was mine.

Alas! My cleansing by the wind was spoilt,

My fast was broken by a drop of wine!

هر روز برانم که کنم شب توبه

از جام و پیالهٔ لبالب توبه

اکنون که رسید وقت گل ترکمده

در موسم گل ز توبه یارب توبه

Each day I promise penance for the night

From cup and brimming goblet of delight;

But now, when roses bloom, grant me release,

Now make, O Lord, penance for penance right.

LXVII

Ah ! with the Grape my fading Life
provide
And wash my Body whence the Life has
died,
   And in a Winding sheet of Vine-leaf
wrapt,
So bury me by some sweet Garden-side.

XCI

Ah, with the Grape my fading Life
provide,
And wash the Body whence the Life
has died,
   And lay me, shrouded in the living
Leaf
By some not unfrequented Garden-side.

LXVIII

That ev'n my buried Ashes such a Snare
Of Perfume shall fling up into the Air,
   As not a True Believer passing by
But shall be overtaken, unaware.

XCII

That ev'n my buried Ashes such a snare
Of Vintage shall fling up into the Air
   As not a True-believer passing by
But shall be overtaken unaware.

LXIX

Indeed, the Idols I have loved so long
Have done my credit in Men's Eye much
    wrong :
   Have drown'd my Honour in a shallow
Cup
And sold my Reputation for a Song.

XCIII

Indeed the Idols I have loved so long
Have done my credit in this World much
    wrong ;
   Have drown'd my Glory in a shallow
Cup
And sold my Reputation for a Song.

LXX

Indeed, indeed, Repentance oft before
I swore—but was I sober when I swore ?
   And then and then came Spring, and
Rose-in-hand
My thread-bare Penitence apieces tore.

XCIV

The same as in 1st edition.

Omar Khayyám | *Paraphrase*

با آنکه شراب پردهٔ ما بدرید
تا جان دارم نخواهم از باده برید
من در عجب ز می فروشان کایشان
به زین که فروشند چه خواهند خرید

Though wine has rent my honour all awry
I'll never part from wine until I die :

Astonished at the wine-sellers am I,

Better than what they sell, what can they buy ?

افسوس که نامهٔ جوانی طی شد
وین تازه بهار ارغوانی دی شد
آن مرغ طرب که نام او بود شباب
افسوس ندانم که کی آمد کی شد

Alas ! the book of forceful youth must close !
My purple spring is changed to winter snows ;
The Bird of mirth whose name was "Prime of Life"
When thrilled its song ? When ceased it ? No one knows.

ای کاش که جای آرمیدن بودی
با این ره دور مرا رسیدن بودی
کاش از پای صد هزار سال از دل خاک
چون سبزه امید بر دمیدن بودی

Ah ! that for respite we might find a room,
Or gain our goal by this long road of gloom !
That after untold years a hope there were
That we like verdure from the earth might bloom !

یزدان خواهم جهان دگرگون کندی
واکنون کندی تانگرم چون کندی
یا نام من از جریده بیرون کندی
یا روزی من از از غیب افزون کندی

Oh ! would that God might alter this world quite !
And do it now that I might see the sight !
That He would cross my name from out His roll,
Or from His store increase my means so slight !

گر بر فلکم دست بدّی چون یزدان
برداشتمی من این فلک را ز میان
از نو فلک دگر چنان ساختمی
کازاده بکام دل رسیدی آسان

If I like God the heavens could constrain,
The same I'd shatter from their tyrant reign ;
And other heav'ns I'd build of such a kind
That thou, made free, thy wishes might attain.

FitzGerald, 1st edition

LXXI
And much as Wine has play'd the Infidel
And robb'd me of my Robe of Honour—
     well,
   I often wonder what the Vintners buy
One half so precious as the Goods they
   sell.

LXXII
Alas! that Spring should vanish with
     the Rose!
That Youth's sweet-scented Manuscript
     should close!
   The Nightingale that in the Branches
   sang,
Ah, whence, and whither flown again,
   who knows!

No parallel.

No parallel.

LXXIII
Ah Love! could thou and I with Fate
     conspire
To grasp this sorry Scheme of Things
     entire,
   Would not we shatter it to bits—and
   then
Re-mould it nearer to the Heart's Desire!

FitzGerald, 4th edition

XCV
And much as Wine has play'd the Infidel,
And robb'd me of my Robe of Honour—
     Well
   I often wonder what the Vintners buy
One half so precious as the stuff they sell.

XCVI
Yet Ah! that spring should vanish with
     the Rose!
That Youth's sweet-scented manuscript
     should close!
   The Nightingale that in the branches
   sang,
Ah whence, and whither flown again,
   who knows!

XCVII
Would but the Desert of the Fountain
     yield
One glimpse—if dimly, yet indeed,
     reveal'd,
   To which the fainting Traveller
   might spring,
As springs the trampled herbage of the
   field!

XCVIII
Would but some wingéd Angel ere too
     late
Arrest the yet unfolded Roll of Fate,
   And make the stern Recorder otherwise
Enregister, or quite obliterate!

XCIX
Ah Love! could you and I with Him
     conspire
To grasp this sorry Scheme of Things
     entire,
   Would not we shatter it to bits—and
   then
Re-mould it nearer to the Heart's Desire!
        *   *   *   *

<table>
<tr><td>Omar Khayyám</td><td>Paraphrase</td></tr>
</table>

چون عهده نمی شود کسی فردا را

حالی خوش کن تو این پرسودا را

می نوش بنور ماه ای ماه که ماه

بسیار بتابد و نیابد مارا

We cannot count upon to-morrow's
    morn,
Now cheer my love-sick heart with
    smarts o'er-borne.
    Ah Moon ! By moon-light drink—for
    oft the moon
Shall seek us long and find our place
    forlorn.

یاران چو باتفاق میعاد کنید

خودرا بجمال یکدگر شاد کنید

ساقی چو می مغانه برکف گیرد

بیچاره فلانرا بدعا یاد کنید

(a)

When you, my friends, in gatherings
    agree
Each others graces, too, rejoice to see,

    And when the Saki brings the Magian
    wine,
Repeat a benison for hapless me.

یاران چو باتفاق دیدار کنید

باید که ز دوست یاد بسیار کنید

چون باده خوشگوار نوشید بهم

نوبت چو بما رسد نگونسار کنید

(b)

When you, my friends, your kindly
    greetings make,
It well behoves old memories to wake ;

    And when you quaff choice wine
    and my turn comes
A cup turn down, for " auld acquaintance
    sake ".

LXXIV
Ah ! Moon of my Delight who know'st
    no wane,
The Moon of Heav'n is rising once again :
    How oft hereafter rising shall she look
Through this same Garden after me—in
    vain !

C
Yon rising Moon that looks for us again—

How oft hereafter will she wax and wane ;
    How oft hereafter rising look for us
Through this same Garden—and for
    one in vain !

LXXV
And when Thyself with shining Foot
    shall pass
Among the Guests Star-scatter'd on the
    Grass,
    And in thy joyous Errand reach the
    Spot
Where I made one—turn down an
    empty Glass !

CI
And when like her, O Saki, you shall
    pass
Among the Guests Star-scatter'd on the
    Grass,
    And in your joyous errand reach the
    spot
Where I made One—turn down an
    empty Glass !

TAMÁM SHUD.   TAMÁM.

A few more examples of quatrains are added.

Omar Khayyám	*Paraphrase*

(1)

چون ابر بنوروز رخ لاله بشست

بر خیز و بجام باده کن عزم درست

کین سبزه که امروز تماشا گهٔ تست

فردا همه از خاک تو بر خواهد رست

When tulips "cheeks" are washed at New Year's day

By clouds in travail, rise without delay,

The goblet fill. This verdure now so fair

Will spring as fair to-morrow from your clay.

(2)

با بط می گفت ماهی درتپ و تاب

باشد که بجوی رفته باز آید آب

بط گفت چون من و توگشتیم کباب

بود از پس مرگ من چه دریا چه سراب

Said a fish near death in the pitiless sun,

"Does a stream refill when it ceases to run?"

Quoth a duck: "What matters the source or the sea

When we are cooked to death and quite undone?"

(3)

آن کس که زمین وچرخ و افلاک نهاد

بس داغ که او بردل غمناک نهاد

بسیار لب چو لعل زلفین چو مشک

در طبل زمین و حقّه خاک نهاد

He who the earth and sky and heavens made

Sore hearts not few with added soreness frayed;

And ruby lips and locks as dark as musk,

In hollow'd earth and chamber'd mould He laid.

(4)

روزی که جزای هر صفت خواهد بود

قدر تو بقدر هرصفت خواهد بود

در حسن صفت کوش که در روز جزا

حشر تو بصورت صفت خواهد بود

In that last day when all shall be repaid

Thy worth on character shall be assayed;

In virtue strive or on that day thy doom

On qualities acquired shall be laid.

(5)

فردا که نصیب نیکبختان بخشند

قسمی بمن رند پریشان بخشند

گر نیک آیم مرا از ایشان شمرند

ور بد باشم مرا بدیشان بخشند

To-morrow when the fortunate are blest

Me, too, a vagabond they will invest;

If I arise as "good" they'll count me so,

As "bad" a special grace shall on me rest.

Omar Khayyám	Paraphrase

(6)

می پرسیدی که چیست این نقش مجاز

گر بر گویم حقیقتش هست دراز

نقشی‌ست پدید آمده از دریا ئی

وانگاه شده بقعر آن دریا باز

Illusion's secret way thou would'st discern,

Not brief at all the story thou must learn.

  The phantom forms that from the ocean came,

Again to depth of ocean must return.

(7)

مرغی دیدم نشسته بر بارهٔ طوس

در پیش نهاده کلّهٔ کیکائوس

با کلّه همی گفت که افسوس افسوس

کو بانگ جرسا و کجا نالهٔ کوس

I saw a vulture on a tower of Tús

That held and scanned the skull of Kaikäús

  The while it cried: "Alas, Alas! Where now

The clash of bells, the rolling of the kús ?"

(8)

فرز این صفتا که مست غمهات شدم

وز اسپ پیاده جفاهات شدم

از بازی فیل و شاه چون در ماندم

رخ بررخ تو نهاده ام مات شدم

Thou Queen ! In love I was inebriate

From Knight reduced by thee to Pawn's estate ;

  When King and Bishop brought me no relief,

My Rook thy Rook opposed, and thou said'st "Mate".

(9)

گل گفت که من یوسف مصرچمنم

یاقوت گران مائهٔ پرزر دهنم

گفتم چو تو یوسفی نشانی بنائی

گفتا که بخون عزقه مگر پیرهنم

"As Joseph I am known," the blush rose said,

My mouth is gold set in a ruby red."

  "As thou art Joseph, give a sign," said I.

Quoth he, "My vesture shows the blood I shed."

(10)

تا بتوانی حدیث رندان می کن

بنیاد فساد دهر ویران میکن

بشنو سخن عمر خیّامی

میمی خور وره میزن واحسان میکن

Hold fast the ancient lore of Dervish-hood,

Of worldly plots destroy the very brood.

  Hark to the words of 'Umar-i-Khayyám

"Drink wine, follow the road, to all do good."

APPENDIX

I

Authorities.—Bye, Ca, P¹, P¹¹¹¹, and R are identical. B, B¹¹, B¹¹¹ are nearly similar. C, C¹, I, I¹ are nearly the same and have in line 2 " pebble " instead of " wine ". There is much diversity in the Arabic word *ishrabu* " drink ye " in l. 4. And A, L, and L¹, which otherwise agree with the text, have here *za sar-i-nau* " from a fresh beginning ", and *za sirr-i-tu* " from thy secret " instead of *ishrabu*. W as text.

> The Sun casts the noose of dawn on the roof,
> The Cyrus of the Day pours wine into the cup ;
> Drink wine, for the Muezzin, rising at dawn,
> Chants forth into the days " Drink ye ".

Notes.—" Roof." There is a play on the words *bám* " roof " and *jám* " cup ". My old Shírází friend pointed out to me that a vaulted roof or dome was probably intended as opposed to an inverted dome or cup. " Moreover," he said, " a noose or loop of light is consistent with a rounded surface."

" Cyrus of the Day." Cf. Hafiz, p. 62. " When the king with his sword scattering golden beams seized the world."

" Wine." The Calcutta version which was the source of FitzGerald's inspiration has " pebble " instead of " wine ". But the poetic image is entirely altered by this one word. On the one hand we have a vision of red and amber clouds as the " Cyrus of the Day " pours wine into the cup of the dawn, and are reminded of Milton's verse in L'Allegro—

> Right against the Eastern gate
> Where the great sun begins his state
> Robed in flames and amber light
> The clouds in thousand liveries dight

and of Homer's " rosy-fingered dawn "—and on the other hand the sun is said to have given the signal for the departure of night. The origin of this expression may be said to lie in the nature of the camel, as my friend pointed out to me. For the camel requires much time for browsing after a march is completed, When, therefore, camels form part of a caravan, a very early start, in the dark, is necessary, and this is, I believe, enjoined in the Kurán. The caravan leader throws a *pebble* into a metal vessel and covering its mouth with his hand uses it as a " rattle ". On his signal the whole company load their animals. FitzGerald followed the Calcutta version and his quatrains, especially that in the 1st Edition, far surpass the original in imagery and beauty.

" Chants." Those who have been accustomed to hear the '*azán* day by day will remember that it is usually given as a high-pitched and musical chant, but there is reason to think that the Arabic *ishrabu* and the Persian *za sar-i-nau* and *za sirr-i-tu* are meant to represent the crowing of a cock, possibly as a sly hit against religion. See Dr. Rosen's Persian edition of 1928.

" Into the days," i.e. Into the world.

II

Authorities.—C, C¹, B¹, B¹¹¹, B¹¹¹¹, Ca, I, L¹, N, A are identical. W is similar.

> One dawning there came a cry from our wine-tavern :
> " O dissolute, tavern-haunting madman,
> Rise, that we may fill our measures with wine
> Before they fill our measure."

FitzGerald's note.—The " False Dawn " ; *Subhi Kázib*, a transient Light on the Horizon about an hour before the *Subhi Sádik*, or True Dawn ; a well-known phenomenon in the East.

Further notes.—It would seem that the worshippers of wine, as the Persian poets often call them, were accustomed to commence the day with wine, for Hafiz in one of his odes refers to the customary three cups of wine as the " triple bath or cleanser ", and in another he refers to the morning " tapsters ". Compare also Isaiah v, 11 : " Woe unto them that rise up early in the morning that they may follow strong drink." As to wine-drinking, we must remember that though the country was dominated by Muslim manners after the Arab invasion of A.D. 641, yet ancient customs survived, and there was a strong prejudice against the Arab invaders and their successors. Thus as late as about A.D. 1000 Firdausi wrote the Sháhnáma, or Book of Kings, using for the most part pure Persian words in its composition,[1] and it is clear that the *Maghs* or " Fire-worshippers ", from whom we get the Latin *Magi* and our *Magician*, were a strong factor in the country. The manufacture of wine seems to have remained almost entirely in their hands, and the best wine was named after them, *Mughána*. Now the Persian poets, acquainted as they were with the circumstances which led to the prohibition of wine, for the most part hid their ideas on the subject in a kind of mystic poetry, so that the Ulema had a saying : " Poetry is heresy." [2]

Some modern Persians regard this quatrain as mystical. The morning draught is said to represent the morning adoration of the Creator. But FitzGerald in his introduction vehemently rebuts the idea that 'Omar was a mystic, and pulverizes the unfortunate M. Nicolas who made the suggestion. Nevertheless, we are much indebted to M. Nicolas, who has indeed opened a window through which we may view Persian poetry as seen by modern mystics.

III

Authorities.—B[111], B[1111], Bye, Ca, L, L[1], A are identical. C, C[1], I, I[1] have in l. 4 " drink the dregs ". N has in l. 4 " leave the traditions *and* austerity ". W is the same as N.

It is the time of the morning draught and of cock-crow, O Saki,
We and wine and the street of the wine-sellers, O Saki.
What place is there for good advice ? Hush, O Saki,
Leave the tradition of austerity and drink, O Saki.

IV

(a)

Authorities.—B, Ca, I, L, L[1], N, A are all identical. O, P[1] and P[1111] have " spring breezes " in l. 1. C[1] has *pardahá* veils in l. 4. W nearly similar.

It is the time when they deck out the world with verdure,
Moses-like (buds) put out their palms from the bough,
Jesus-breathing (herbs) break forth from the ground,
Against the eye of the clouds they open their eyes.

(b)

Authorities.—O, P[1], and P[1111] are identical. W as text.

Now that the world is won back (from winter) for happiness
That folk with " souls " have a yearning towards the pastures,
On every bough is the sheen of Moses' hand,
In every breath of wind is the call of Jesus' breath.

FitzGerald's note.—New Year, beginning with the vernal equinox it must be remembered ; and (however, the old solar year is practically superseded by the *clumsy* Lunar Year, that dates from the Mohammedan Hijra) still commemorated by a Festival

---

[1] Professor M. Mahfuz-ul-Haq, of the Presidency College, Calcutta, has pointed out that the proportion of Arabic words in the Sháhnáma is about 7 per cent, and refers to Professor Browne on the subject.
[2] [I believe that the saying *Ash-sh'ar bad'aa* is a hadith of Muhammad.—W. H.]

that is said to have been appointed by the very Jamshýd whom Omar so often talks of, and whose yearly calendar he helped to rectify. "The sudden approach and rapid advance of Spring," says Mr. Binning,[1] "are very striking. Before the snow is well off the ground, the trees burst into bloom and the flowers start forth from the soil. At *Now Rooz* (their New Year's Day) the snow was lying in patches on the hills and in the shaded valleys, while the fruit trees in the gardens were budding beautifully, and green plants and flowers springing up on the plains on every side.

> 'And on old Hyem's Chin and icy Crown
> An odorous Chaplet of sweet Summer buds
> Is, as in mockery, set—.'

Among the plants newly appeared I recognized some old acquaintances I had not seen for many a year : among these, two varieties of the thistle, a coarse species of daisy like the Horse-gowan, red and white clover, the dock, the blue corn-flower, and that vulgar herb, the dandelion, rearing its yellow crest on the banks of the water-courses." The nightingale was not yet heard, for the rose was not yet blown ; but an almost identical blackbird and woodpecker helped to make up something of a north-country spring.

"The White Hand of Moses," Exodus iv, 6, where Moses draws forth his hand, not according to the Persians *leprous as snow*, but white as our May blossom in Spring perhaps. According to them also the Healing Power of Jesus resided in his breath.

Further notes.—As to Moses, see Kurán, s. lv. There is a Muhammadan tradition that Moses was a *black* man.

"Hands," lit. palms. Some translators have given the word *kaf* the meaning of "froth", a meaning which it possesses, but let us remember that in the Jewish and Muhammadan act of prayer the palms are held up to receive a blessing. In Persian the words meaning "possessing the breath of Jesus" and "possessing the breath of the Anointed, or Christ" are synonyms.

V

FitzGerald's notes.—Iram planted by the King Shaddád, and now sunk somewhere in the sands of Arabia. Jamshýd's seven-ringed cup was typical of the seven heavens, seven planets, seven seas, etc., and was a *Divining Cup*.

Further notes.—As to Iram (not Irám as in the 1st edition) compare Kurán, s. lxxxix, also Hafiz, pp. 53 and 376. According to Doughty "the City of Columns, the terrestrial paradise" was a few miles westward of the old pilgrim track near Khurbet-er-Rum (Roman ruins) not far from Akaba, where are found many ancient pillars. See *Arabia Deserta*.

VI

Authorities.—B, Ca, L, L¹, N, R are identical (B and N in l. 3 defective). O, P¹, and P¹¹¹¹ have in l. 3 "in the Pahlavi tongue". A nearly the same. W the same as text.

> The day is fine, the air is neither hot nor cold,
> The clouds wash the dust from the cheeks of the roses,
> The nightingale complains in its own tongue to the yellow rose
> We must drink wine.

FitzGerald's notes.—Pehlevi, the old Heroic Sanskrit of Persia. Háfiz also speaks of the Nightingale's Pehlevi, which did not change with the People's. I am not sure if the fourth line refers to the red rose looking sickly, or to the yellow rose that ought to be red ; red, white, and yellow roses are common in Persia. I think that Southey in his common-place book quotes from some Spanish author about the rose being white till 10 o'clock ; "Rosa Perfecta" at 2 ; and "perfecta incarnada" at 5.

Further notes.—O, P¹, and P¹¹¹¹ are, I think, alone in mentioning the Pahlavi language, which, how-ever, FitzGerald was not quite right in supposing to be a kind of Sanskrit. Háfiz represents the nightingale as lecturing the rose from a book called *Mukamát-i-M'anavi*, pp. 160 and 327.

[1] *Two Years' Travel in Persia*, etc., i, 165.

F

VII

Authorities.—B^{1111}, Bye, Ca, L, L^1, A are identical. C, C^1, B, B^{111}, I, I^1 all have slight differences. W as text.

Every day I am disposed to do penance in the evening,
Penance from the cup and brimming goblet;
Now that the season of roses has come grant me release,
In the season of roses (grant) O Lord penance for (the intention) of penance.

Note.—Compare Háfiz, p. 74.

VIII (1st Edition)

Authorities.—B^{11}, B^{111}, B^{1111}, I, L, L^1 (defective), P^1 are identical. B has in l. 1 *hangám-i-subh* "it is morning time". C^1 and I^1 are nearly similar. N, R, A, and P^{1111} have in l. 2 *bar sáz* instead of *pur sáz* with the same meaning. W agrees with N.

It is time for the morning draught, Idol of happy feet!
Play loudly on the harp, and bring forth wine.
For this coming of the month of Tír (spring) and the departure of Dai (December)
Has cast away in the dust one hundred thousand Jams (Jamshids) and Kais.

Note.—*Tír*, a month of Spring. *Kais*, Kings of the Kai dynasty.

VIII (4th Edition)

Authorities.—There is much diversity in the text of this quatrain, but not in the meaning. B^{111}, L^1, and A are identical. B^{11} very nearly similar. O, C^1, Bye, Ca, I, I^1, L, N, P^1, P^{1111}, and R all vary. Ca and N have in l. 1 "when the soul is at the lips". W as N.

Since life passes away what matters it if it be sweet or bitter?
When the measure is filled what matters Baghdad or Balkh?
Drink wine—for after thee and me the moon shall often
Pass from the day of full moon to the first day of the moon, and from new to full moon.

Note.—FitzGerald's Naishápúr was taken from Nicolas. FitzGerald is quite correct, but the name is constantly written and pronounced "Nishapur". My old friend insisted that the word was Naishápúr, and that it was derived from *nai* "reeds" and *Sháhpúr* "the King".
Salkh denotes stripping off the skin and is the name of a well-known and very fearful Arabian ceremony, as mentioned by Burton. It is used to denote the day of full moon. *Gharra* signifies the first day of the moon.

IX

Authorities.—C, B, B^1, I, I^1, L^1, N, P^1, R, and A are identical. B^{1111} and L nearly similar. W as text.

With the coming of spring and the passing of winter
The leaves of our existence are folded.
Drink wine and be not sad, a sage has said:
"Griefs are like poison and their antidote is wine."

IX AND X

Authorities.—B, B^{1111}, L^1, N, P^{11}, R, A are identical. C, I, I^1 are nearly the same. P^{1111} differs widely and deprecates trespassing outside the door of a wine tavern. W as text.

Whilst thou hast in thy body bones and sinews and veins
Put not thy foot beyond the dwelling-place of thy Fate.
If Rustam, son of Zál, is opposed to thee yield not thy neck,
Accept no favour if Hátim Tai be thy friend.

FitzGerald's notes.—Rustum the Hercules of Persia and Zál, his father, whose exploits are among the most celebrated in the Sháhnáma. Hátim Tai, a well-known type of Oriental generosity.

X AND XI

(*a*)

Authorities.—There is great diversity in this quatrain. Bye, L¹, and A are identical. O, C¹, B¹¹¹, B¹¹¹¹, Ca, I, L, N, P, P¹¹¹¹, R vary. W nearly the same as text.

I am not at all aware whether He who created me
Made me from folk of heaven, or horrible hell.
A cup and a mistress and a lute on the bank of a sown field,
These three are present cash for me. Thine be the promised heaven !

Note.—" Bank." The fields are commonly irrigated terraces and are bounded on the lower side by banks composed of stones picked from the fields, which in spring are covered with flowers.

(*b*)

Authorities.—B, L, P¹¹¹¹ are identical. O, C¹, B¹, B¹¹, B¹¹¹, I, I¹, L¹, N, P¹, P¹¹, R all nearly similar. A has in l. 3 " sitting in a garden ". W nearly similar.

If I am so lucky as to have a loaf made from the kernels of wheat
And a gourd of wine, and a leg of mutton,
And if I be sitting in the wilderness with one whose face is beautiful as the moon,
That would be a happiness beyond the reach of a Sultan.

Note.—" Bread of wheat ", from the kernels of wheat, from wheat of the same kind as that from which macaroni is made. Cf. Moses' song, Deut. xxxii, 14, " with the fat of the kidneys of wheat " ; also Psalms lxxxi, 16, and cxlvii, 14. FitzGerald's " Thou beside me singing " is derived according to Mr. Heron-Allen from the mention of a lute in the preceding quatrain, Calcutta version.

XII AND XIII

Authorities.—O, P, P¹¹¹, P¹¹¹¹ are identical. B, I¹, R are also identical and form another group similar in meaning. C¹, Bye, I, L, L¹, P¹ vary a good deal. W as text.

They tell me the Garden of Eden is delightful with Houris,
I say the juice of the grape is delightful.
Take ready money, and put credit aside,
The sound of the drum, Brother, from afar is pleasing.

FitzGerald's note.—A drum beaten outside a palace.

Further note.—My Persian friend explained that the drum signified the drum sounding at the last day. I said, " Are you sure there will be a drum ? " He answered : " According to the Kurán a trumpet will sound. But if there are trumpets, there will also be drums." The expression in the Kurán is " stunning trumpet blast ", s. lxxx.

XIII AND XIV

Authorities.—C, C¹, I, I¹ are all identical. Not in W.

The rose said : I brought a hand scattering gold,
Laughing, laughing I blew into the world.
I untied the string from the end of my purse and departed,
Every coin that I had I scattered around me.

FitzGerald's note.—That is the rose's golden centre.

XIV AND XVI

Authorities.—Bye and L identical. B¹¹¹, B¹¹¹¹, Ca almost the same. C, C¹, I, I¹, L¹ differ a good deal. R quite different in ll. 3 and 4. Not in W.

> Assume the whole world from end to end covered with longed-for gold,
> That a hundred hoards sparkle with gold and gems.
> Then assume that as an end of such hoards, like as snow
> Remains a day or two on the desert, they melt away.

Note.—This is one of Zukowski's so-called "wandering quatrains" and is found in Sháhi Ákifi, and is No. 154 in Zukowski's list. See Dr. Rosen's article in the *Zeitschrift der Deutschen Morgenländischen Gesellschaft*, Band 5, Heft 3, 1926.

XV

Authorities.—O, Bye, P¹¹¹¹ identical. B¹¹, B¹¹¹, L, P, P¹, R almost identical with text. C, I, I¹, L¹, N, P¹, A all have in l. 1 "before thy griefs bring a night attack on thee". B alone has "before Princes murder thee". W is the same as text.

> Before men attack thee at night,
> Bid wine be brought of rosy colour;
> Thou are not gold, O careless fool! that men
> Should bury thee in the earth and again bring thee forth.

XVI AND XVII

Authorities.—C, C¹ (defective), B, B¹, B¹¹, Ca, I (defective), I¹ (defective), L, L¹, P¹, R, A are all identical. B¹¹¹ and N have in l. 4 "It is a grave". W the same as B¹¹¹ and N.

> This ancient Inn that they call the world
> Is the stable of the piebald horse of morning and night,
> It is a feast left over by a hundred Jamshids,
> It is a palace, the pillowed resting-place of one hundred Bahráms.

Note.—"Ancient Inn", Háfiz, has the same expression for the world, p. 107.

XVII AND XVIII

Authorities.—C, C¹, B¹¹, B¹¹¹¹, Bye, Ca, I, I¹, L are identical. B¹ almost the same. B¹¹¹, L¹, N, R, A have in l. 3 "The gazelle has dropped its fawn". P, P¹, P¹¹ have "The gazelle rests therein". T has Jamshíd instead of Bahrám in l. 1. W as N.

> That palace wherein Bahrám held the cup
> The fox has whelped (in it) and the lion rests (therein).
> Bahrám who was continually catching wild asses (gúr)
> Lo! To-day the grave (gúr) has caught Bahrám.

FitzGerald's notes.—Persepolis: called also *Takht-i-Jamshyd*. THE THRONE OF JAMSHÝD, *King Splendid* of the mythical *Peshdadian* Dynasty, and supposed (according to the Sháhnáma) to have been founded and built by him. Others refer it to the work of the Genie King, Ján Ibn Ján, who also built the Pyramids before the time of Adam.

Bahrám Gúr, *Bahrám of the Wild Ass*, a Sassanian sovereign, had also his seven castles (like the King of Bohemia) each of a different colour; each with a Royal Mistress within; each of whom tells a story, as told in one of the most famous poems of Persia, written by Amir Khusraw: all these seven, also figuring (according to Eastern Mysticism) the seven heavens; and perhaps the book itself that eighth, into which the mystical seven transcend, and within which they revolve. The ruins of three of those towers are yet shown by the peasantry; as also the swamp in which Bahrám sunk, like the Master of Ravenswood, while pursuing his *Gúr*.

> The Palace that to heav'n his pillars threw
> And kings the forehead on his threshold drew
>   I saw the solitary ring-dove there
> And " Coo, coo, coo " she cried; and " Coo, coo, coo ".

This quatrain Mr. Binning found among several of Háfiz and others, inscribed by some stray hand among the ruins of Persepolis. The ring-dove's ancient *Pehlevi Coo, coo, coo* signifies also in Persian *Where? Where? Where?* In Attár's *Bird-parliament* she is reproved by the leader of the birds for sitting still, and for ever harping on that note of lamentation for her lost Yúsuf.

Apropos of Omar's red roses in Stanza xix I am reminded of an old English superstition that our anemone *Pulsatilla*, or purple " Pasque flower " (which grows plentifully about the Fleam Dyke, near Cambridge) grows only where Danish blood has been spilt.

Further notes.—There is a play on the word *gúr*, which means equally " wild ass " or " grave ". And there is a further play, for the *gúr* which Bahrám so continually hunted, as " grave " lay in wait for him, as it were hunter-wise, and he was suddenly engulfed. This is one of Zukowski's so-called " wandering quatrains " and is found in Háfiz. It is No. 13 in Zukowski's list. Dr. Rosen strongly protests that it is a genuine piece of Omar's work. See Dr. Rosen's article in the *Zeitschrift der Deutschen Morgenländischen Gesellschaft.*

XVIII AND XIX

Authorities.—C¹, Bye, Ca, I¹, L, L¹ (defective), P, A are identical. R is very nearly the same. O and R have in l. 1 " rose and tulip bed ". P¹¹¹¹ has in l. 3 " that grows out of the lawn ". B¹¹¹ is quite different in ll. 3 and 4. W almost the same as O.

> In every desert where a patch of tulips is found,
> This flower comes from the blood of a monarch;
> Each leaf of the violet that grows out of the ground
> Is a mole that has been on the cheek of a beautiful lady.

Note.—FitzGerald's " rose " is from the Ouseley version.

XIX AND XX

Authorities.—C, N, and P¹¹ (defective) are identical. C¹, B, I, I¹, P¹, P¹¹¹¹ are almost exactly the same as the foregoing. B¹¹¹, Bye, Ca, L, L¹, R and A are slightly different. W as text.

> All the verdure that grows on the banks of a water-course
> Grows, as you may say, from the lip of a lady of angelic disposition.
> Beware! tread not roughly on the herbage,
> For the same has grown from the dust of one who had cheeks red as a tulip.

XX AND XXI

Authorities.—B¹¹, B¹¹¹, L, L¹, A are identical. B, N, P¹, and R¹ are almost simila to the foregoing, but have in l. 4 " we shall be travelling companions ". C, C¹, I, and P are slightly different. W as B and N.

Come friend ! Let us not worry about to-morrow,
And let us make the most of this momentary life.
To-morrow when we pass from this ancient abode
We shall be cheek by jowl with those of seven thousand years ago.

FitzGerald's note.—A thousand years to each planet.

XXI AND XXII

Authorities.—C, C¹, B¹¹¹, I are all identical. B, B¹¹, B¹¹¹¹, Ca, L, L¹, A all vary
slightly. B¹¹ has in l. 3 *sharáb-khwár* " wine-drinkers ". W nearly as text.

All my dear friends have departed,
One by one they have been trodden down under Death's feet.
They were gathered together to a wine-party in Life's assembly,
A round or two before us they became intoxicated.

Note.—The admirable skill displayed by FitzGerald in his treatment of Omar's very dull quatrain
may be noted.

XXII AND XXIII

(*a*)

Authorities.—*Shádkámi* in l. 2 of C is probably a mistake for *shádmáni*. If so,
then C, C¹, B, Bye (defective), L¹, P¹, P¹¹, R are identical. B¹¹¹, Ca, I¹, L (defective),
N are also identical, and have l. 2 " be content and make a moment pass with merri-
ment ". W as N.

Arise, and do not worry about this fleeting world,
Sit still and merrily let the world pass.
If there were constancy in the nature of the world
Thy (lucky) turn would never come to thee from others.

(*b*)

Authorities.—B (defective), B¹, B¹¹¹, Bye, I, I¹ are all identical. C, C¹, Ca, L, L¹,
N, P¹, P¹¹¹¹, R nearly similar. W the same as text.

The clouds came and again shed tears on the verdure,
(And) without purple wine we must not live.
This verdure that delights our eyes to-day (shall remain)
Until the verdure (nourished) from our dust shall delight the eyes of whom
we know not.

This is one of Zukowski's so-called " wandering quatrains " and is found in Háfiz. It is No. 9 in
Zukowski's list. There is no reason to think it is not genuine. See Dr. Rosen's article in the *Zeitschrift
der Deutschen Morgenländischen Gesellschaft*, 1926.

XXIII AND XXIV

Authorities.—C¹, B¹¹, B¹¹¹, Ca, L, L¹, A are identical. O, B, B¹¹¹¹, P, P¹ are nearly
similar with the foregoing and recommend a mistress' lips, a book and wine on the bank
of a stream. P¹¹¹¹ recommends a house on the bank of a stream, etc. Not in W.

Allow no grief (or passion) to hold thee in its castle,
Nor vain regrets to dominate thy days.
Drink wine on the grassy bank of a stream
Before the time when the earth shall embrace thee.

XXIV AND XXV

Authorities.—C, C[1], B, I, L, L[1], N, P[1], P[11], A are all identical. W as text.

Some folk are absorbed in thoughts about doctrine and faith;
A crowd is confused as to what is doubtful and what is certain.
Suddenly a Muezzin cries out (comes forth) from his lurking place,
" Fools ! The road is neither this nor that."

Note.—The word *kamin* means an ambush or lurking place and is not easily associated with a minaret or tower from whence a Muezzin usually chants the *dzán*, but here the word includes the idea of the darkness of early dawn ; whence we get FitzGerald's masterly " Tower of Darkness ".
This is one of Zukowski's so-called " wandering quatrains " and is found in Sháh Sanján. It is No. 250 in Zukowski's list. See Dr. Rosen's article in the *Zeitschrift der Deutschen Morgenländischen Gesellschaft*, 1926.

XXV AND XXVI

Authorities.—O, B, B[11], B[1111], Ca, L[1], N, P, P[1], A are all identical. C, C[1], I, I[1], L nearly the same. Bye different. W as text.

Those who have gone before, O Saki,
Have slept in the dust of their pride, O Saki,
Go and drink wine, and hear the truth from me,
All that they have said is wind, O Saki.

Note.—As shown above the Ouseley version reads : " have slept in the dust of their pride ", whence we get FitzGerald's intensified : " their mouths are stopt with dust."

XXVI (1st Edition)

Authorities.—O, C, C[1], I, I[1], L, L[1], P[1], P[1111] are all identical. B[1], B[111], Bye read " without wine " in l. 2. W as text.

Drink wine. For thou shalt sleep under the clay many a day,
Without a companion, without a fellow, without an intimate friend or wife ;
Beware thou divulge not this hidden mystery to anyone,
" The withered tulip shall never bloom again."

XXVII AND XXVIII

(a)

Authorities.—Ca, L, L[1] identical. B and A almost exactly the same. O, P[1111] have in l. 4 " like water ". P has in l. 4 " we came as a cloud ". W as text.

In boyhood we spent some time with a master,
We were quite pleased with our learning ;
Look at the end of the story, what happened to us (to learn),
" We came from the dust—and we went like the wind ".

Note.—As shown above, the Ouseley version whence FitzGerald took his inspiration reads : " we came like water."

(b)

Authorities.—C, C[1], I, I[1] are identical. N and R almost the same. B, B[11], B[111], B[1111] vary a good deal. L, L[1], P[1], A have in l. 2 " thou sittest on high ". W the same as N.

I was a falcon (or hawk) and I flew from the world of mystery
That I might make my way with thee from the low to the sublime.
When I found no one here acquainted with the secret
I returned by the same door by which I had come.

Note.—This very curious quatrain would seem to anticipate the author's demise, as if his soul were addressing his body at the moment of death. C, C¹, Ca, N, P¹ all have the unclassical expression *tá bu* in l. 2, but B, B¹¹¹, B¹¹¹¹, L, I, I¹ all have the perfectly grammatical *bá tu* " with thee ". L¹ has the impossible *bu tá*. But L, L¹, and P¹ go a step further and have " thou sittest on high ". The poetical image is probably taken from falconry, and this seems the more probable as 'Omar was the author of a treatise on that art. See Dr. Fr. Rosen's book, *The Quatrains of Omar Khayyám*, Methuen, London, 1930. I hope I may not tire the reader by going a little further in a matter that interests me. As regards the capture of the young of the Saker (Latin *sacer* from the Arabic *sakar*) so well known in India, from the precipices of the Jebal Ethlib near Medain Sálih, see Doughty's *Arabia Deserta*, vol. i, p. 362. The young birds are taken from the nest when the brown feathers have replaced the down. They are then " housed " in a quiet shelter and the bells or *jesses* attached. The parent birds are noted for courage and devotion to their young, and doubtless endeavour to rescue them, whence the poetical image.

This quatrain is one of Zukowski's so-called " wandering quatrains " and is found in Ansári, 'Attár, and Muhammad Hassan Khán. It is No. 171 in Zukowski's list. See Dr. Rosen's article in the *Zeitschrift der Deutschen Morgenländischen Gesellschaft*, 1926.

(c)

Authorities.—C¹, B¹, B¹¹, B¹¹¹, B¹¹¹¹, I, N, A are all identical. P nearly similar. L and L¹ have in l. 1 " if ", probably a slip of the pen. O and B are slightly different. W as text.

No one has solved the mysteries of beginningless eternity,
No one has trespassed a pace beyond his natural powers ;
From Acolyte I (must) look to the Master.
Impotence resides in the hand of everyone born of a mother.

XXIX

Authorities.—C, C¹, B, B¹¹, B¹¹¹, Bye, I, I¹, L, L¹, N, A are all identical. W as text.

At the first He brought me into existence confusedly,
Nothing increased (or grew) in me except amazement at life ;
We journeyed on in disgust. We know not what was
The meaning of this coming and being and (then) departing.

XXX

Authorities.—O, C¹, B¹, B¹¹¹, B¹¹¹¹, Bye, I, I¹, L, L¹, A, P¹¹¹¹ are all identical. B has ll. 2 and 3 transposed. W as text.

Since my coming was uninfluenced by me on the day of creation,
And my departure, so undesired, is firmly fixed,
Arise and gird thyself, smart cup bearer,
For I will wash away the worries of the world with wine.

XXXI

Authorities.—C¹, B¹¹¹¹, Bye, Ca, I (defective), P¹¹¹¹ all identical. C, B, B¹, B¹¹¹, I¹, A vary slightly. W as text.

From the nether globe of the earth to the height of Saturn,
I solved all the difficulties of the Universe ;
I leaped forth from the bonds of every (kind of) deception and artifice.
Every obstacle was cleared away—except that of death.

FitzGerald's note.—Saturn, Lord of the Seventh Heaven.

XXXII

(a)

Authorities.—C, C[1], B[111], Bye, I, L[1], P[1], P[1111], R are all identical. I[1], L, A are almost the same as the foregoing. W as text.

Neither thou nor I understand the secrets of eternity (without beginning)
And this enigma neither thou canst read nor I;
There is a talk of me and thee behind the veil,
But when the veil is drawn thou wilt not exist, nor I.

Note.—This is one of Zukowski's so-called "wandering quatrains" and is found in Abul Hussan-i-Khirquáni. It is No. 240 in Zukowski's list. See Dr. Rosen's article in the *Zeitschrift der Deutschen Morgenländischen Gesellschaft*, 1926.

(b)

Authorities.—B, B[1111], N are identical. C, C[1], I are also identical, forming a second group. Ca, L, L[1], A form a third group. The second and third groups have in ll. 3 and 4, "Everyone has made a guess, etc." W as first group.

No one has found a road behind the veil of Fate,
And no one is aware of the secrets of God.
Two and seventy years I meditated night and day,
And found no solution—and the story (of my endeavours) was not short.

Note.—We may mark with what skill FitzGerald has brought out the "me" and "thee" of the text.

XXXIII (4th Edition)

Note.—Mr. Heron-Allen in his Rubá'iyát, 1899, to which I am much indebted for help in obscure parallelism is of opinion that this quatrain was derived from Attár's *Parliament of Birds*.

XXXIII AND XXXIV

Note.—These quatrains also are attributed to Attár's *Parliament of Birds* by Mr. Heron-Allen.

XXXIV AND XXXV

Authorities.—B[1], B[111], Bye, Ca, L, L[1], P[1111], A are identical. O, C[1], B, B[11], B[1111], I, I[1], P, P[1], R vary a good deal. O, which was the source of FitzGerald's inspiration, is closely reproduced in his quatrain xxxv. W is the same as O.

In great desire I held my lip to the lip of a jug,
In order to ask the cause of length of days.
To me it spoke in its own language and told me secretly
"A whole life-time I was such as thou art. Bear with me a moment."

XXXV AND XXXVI

Authorities.—C[1], B, Bye, I[1], L, L[1] (defective), N, P[1], R, A are identical. O, P, P[1111] have in l. 2 "was in pursuit of a beauty". W as text.

This jug like me was once a plaintive lover
And was enthralled by the ends of the curls of a fair lady.
This handle that thou see-est upon its neck
Is an arm that lay on the neck of a sweetheart.

Note.—"Sweetheart." The word *ydr* "friend" often has this meaning in poetry. We may mark with what admirable skill this quatrain has been woven by FitzGerald into a connected whole with the quatrain next before it and that next after it, and let us remember that in the original there is no connection whatever.

XXXVI AND XXXVII

Authorities.—O, C¹, I, N, P, P¹, P¹¹, P¹¹¹¹, R, A are identical. B¹¹, B¹¹¹¹, Bye, I¹, L, L¹ vary slightly. W as text.

> Yesterday I saw a Potter in the market place
> He was kneading roughly with his feet a lump of fresh clay,
> And the clay was saying in the language of its circumstances,
> " I used to be such an one as thou art. Treat me gently."

FitzGerald's note.—One of the Persian poets, Attár I think, has a pretty story about this. A thirsty traveller dips his hand into a spring of water to drink from. By and by comes another who draws up and drinks from an earthen bowl, and then departs, leaving his bowl behind him. The first traveller takes it up for another draught, but is surprised to find that the same water which had tasted sweet from his own hand tastes bitter from the earthen bowl. But a Voice from Heaven, I think, tells him the clay from which the bowl is made was once *man*, and with whatever shape renewed can never lose the bitter flavour of mortality.

XXXVII (1st Edition)

Authorities.—C¹, B, B¹, B¹¹¹, Bye, I, L, L¹, R, A are identical. Ca, I¹, and P are very nearly similar to the foregoing. P¹, P¹¹, and P¹¹¹ have in l. 1 " the new year's zephyr is sweet ". W as text.

> On the face of the rose the new year's dew is sweet,
> On the parterre of the lawn the face of the heart-kindler is sweet;
> Of yesterday that is past all that you say is not sweet.
> Be content. Say nothing of yesterday—for to-day is sweet.

XXXVIII (4th Edition)

(*a*)

Authorities.—The text of the different versions is much spoilt by Scribes' errors, misprints, etc. E.g. C has *sáiya* " shade" for, *pdiya* " tread of wheel " ; C¹ has *jái* " place for ", *rái* " meditation ". L, A have *istáda* " stood " for, *ustád* " master ". B¹¹¹¹, Ca, L, L¹ may, however, be considered identical. P¹¹¹¹ is the same except that it has *pala* for *pdiya*. C, C¹, I, I¹, N, P¹, A vary a good deal. N, P¹ and R have in l. 3 " the *bold* potter ". W as N.

> I pondered in a Potter's workshop,
> I saw the Master-Potter with his foot on the tread of his wheel.
> He was making a handle and a lid for a jar and a jug,
> From the skull of a king and from a beggar's hand.

(*b*)

Authorities.—B, B¹¹¹, Bye, L (defective), L¹, R are identical. P¹, A almost the same. W nearly the same.

> I visited a Potter the other day,
> Every moment showed some (wondrous) skill in clay ;
> I saw, if those devoid of vision saw it not,
> My Father's clay on the hands of every potter.

Note.—The Lucknow version has a note that " my father's clay " means the cla of Adam, and that t he spectator might infer that his own clay would in due course be similarly treated.

XXXIX (4TH EDITION)

Authorities.—O, P, P¹, P¹¹¹¹, R are identical. Bye, Ca, L are also identical and nearly similar to foregoing. C¹, B, B¹¹, B¹¹¹, B¹¹¹¹, I, L¹, N, A vary. N alone has in l. 1 " into the cup ". W as N.

> Every drop the Saki scatters on the ground
> May quench the fire of misery in some burning eye;
> Praise be to God ! Thou thinkest wine a water
> That may free thy heart from a hundred pangs.

FitzGerald's note.—The custom of throwing wine on the ground before drinking still continues in Persia, and perhaps generally in the East. M. Nicolas considers it " un signe de liberalité, et en même temps un avertissement que le buveur doit vider sa coupe jusqu'à la dernière goutte ". Is it not more likely an ancient superstition ; a libation to propitiate earth, or make her an accomplice in the illicit revel ? Or, perhaps, to divert the jealous eye by some sacrifice of superfluity, as with the ancients of the West ? With Omar we see something more is signified ; the precious liquor is not lost, but sinks into the ground to refresh the dust of some poor wine-worshipper foregone. Thus Háfiz copying Omar in so many ways : " When thou drinkest wine pour a draught on the ground. Wherefore fear that sin that brings to another gain ? "

Further note.—We may notice in this quatrain a hidden reference to the four elements, one in each line : thus in l. 1 *khák* " earth ", in l. 2 *átish* " fire ", in l. 3 *bdd(a)* " air ", in l. 4 *db* " water ". This is an instance of that literary subtlety in which Persian poets delight. Seeing that M. Nicolas has " cup " in l. 1, his reference to the ancient custom of throwing wine on the " ground " would seem to be a *non sequitur*.

XL (4TH EDITION)

Authorities.—C, C¹, Bye, I, L are identical. B¹, I¹, L¹, N, A vary somewhat. N has in l. 4 " as a gust of wind ". W the same as N.

Like a tulip on New Year's Day grasp a bowl in thy hand
In company with one who has cheeks like a tulip ; if thou hast the opportunity.
Drink wine merrily. For this worn-out sphere
Shall suddenly turn thee down like a clod of earth.

Note.—The poetic image of the last line is probably taken from the ploughman's share, turning down the soil with the flowers growing on it.

XLI (4TH EDITION)

Authorities.—O, Ca, L (defective), L¹ (defective), P¹¹¹¹ are identical. C¹, I, N, A vary a good deal. R slightly different. W as N.

> Limit thy desire for worldly things and live content,
> And sever thy dependence on the good and evil of the times.
> Take wine and play with the tresses of a heart-enslaver,
> For soon shall pass also and not remain these few days.

XLII (4TH EDITION)

Authorities.—There is great diversity in ll. 1 and 3. B, B¹, B¹¹¹¹, Bye, Ca, L, L¹, P¹¹¹¹ all have in l. 1 " if thou dost worship wine ". B¹¹, B¹¹¹, I and I¹ all have in the same place " if thou art inebriated with love ". O, C¹, B, B¹, B¹¹, B¹¹¹, B¹¹¹¹, Ca, Bye, I, I¹, L, L¹, N, P, P¹, P¹¹, R, A are all nearly similar in ll. 2 and 4 and have the same meaning. The text is from Bye, and B¹¹¹¹ which are identical. W as text.

Khayyám, if thou dost worship wine, rejoice.
If thou are seated by one beautiful as the moon, rejoice.
Since in the end thou wilt perish
Think that thou art not whilst thou art—rejoice.

Note.—This quatrain is one among others that Professor A. Christensen, of Copenhagen, has critically considered. It is No. 6 in a list of quatrains beginning with the name " Khayyám ". Dr. Rosen considers it a genuine quatrain of Omar's. See Dr. Rosen's article in the *Zeitschrift der Deutschen Morgenländischen Gesellschaft*, 1926.

XLIII (4TH EDITION)

Authorities.—C, C^1, B^1, B^{11}, B^{1111}, Ca, I, I^1 are identical. L, L^1, and A have ll. 2 and 4 transposed. W almost the same as the text.

In the circle of the sphere of unfathomable ideas,
There is a cup that they cause all to taste in turn.
When thy turn comes, do not sigh.
Drink without shrinking for thy turn is by compulsion.

FitzGerald's note.—According to one beautiful Oriental legend Azräel accomplishes his mission by holding to the nostril an Apple from the Tree of Life. This and the two following stanzas would have been withdrawn as somewhat *de trop*, from the text, but for advice which I least like to disregard.

Further note.—We may surmise that FitzGerald's " invite your soul forth to your lips " is an echo of " when the soul is at the lips " which appears in N (and Ca), see *Authorities* for VIII (4th edition).

XLIV (4TH EDITION)

Authorities.—O, N, P^{1111} are identical. C^1, B, I, L, L^1, P^1 (defective), A vary slightly. W as text.

O soul ! If thou are purified from the dust of the body
Thou shalt become a solitary spirit in the heavens ;
The empyrean is thy mansion. Shame on thee !
That comest and dost dwell in a tenement of clay.

Note.—" O soul ! " This translation is probably correct in this case. But our expression " Dear heart ! " is usually nearer the meaning.

XLV (4TH EDITION)

Authorities.—C^1, B^1, B^{11}, B^{111}, Ca, I are identical. C, B, B^{1111}, Bye, I^1, L^1, N, P, P^{1111}, A vary. C, B^{1111}, L^1, N, A have in l. 2 " the realm of death ". P and P^{1111} have defective readings in l. 4 for *zanau* ? " again ". W as N.

Khayyám, thy body is exactly like a tent;
Thy soul is a Sultán, and his halting place is the imperishable city.
The Chamberlain, Death, for another stage
Strikes the tent, when the Sultán has arisen.

Note.—The poetic image is that of a Sultán who is journeying to his capital, the imperishable city of God, *dar-i-baká*. Cf. xxvii and xliv above (" I came as Falcon," etc., and " O soul ! " etc.). The Calcutta variant, which was the source of FitzGerald's inspiration, and also B^{1111}, L^1, N, A have instead of the " imperishable city " " the realm of death ", but the majority is in favour of the former reading.

Dr. Fr. Rosen in his article, " Zur Textfrage der Vierzeiler Omar's des Zeltmachers," published in the *Zeitschrift der Deutschen Morgenländischen Gesellschaft*, Band 5, Heft 3, 1926, states that he has found the probable original of this verse in a seemingly old MS. of Jaláluddin's Diván, Shams-i-Tabrizi, which appears to have been written about the year A.D. 1500. He is of opinion that a later copyist may have substituted Khayyám's name in the beginning of the quatrain and made other alterations and ascribed it to Khayyám. He is puzzled by the " nine tents ", but I think *zanau* " again " is intended.

However this may be, it seems possible that the copying may have been done by the writer of the Shams-i-Tabrizi.

XLVI (4TH EDITION)

Authority.—Nicolas. W as text.

Khayyám! Although the blue pavilion of heaven
Has pitched its tent and shut the door on discussion,
Like the form of bubbles of wine in the cup of existence,
The Eternal Saki has shown forth a thousand Khayyáms.

Note.—" And holds it peace ". Cf. Psalm xix : " There is neither speech nor language, but their voices are heard among them " ; and " In them hath he set a Tabernacle for the sun ".
This quatrain is one of those that Professor A. Christensen has noted as beginning with the poet's name. Dr. Rosen is of opinion that its form throws some doubt upon its genuineness. May not 'Omar have in part taken its form from the Psalm I have quoted, through a not improbable Arabic translation ? See Dr. Rosen's article in the *Zeitschrift der Deutschen Morgenländischen Gesellschaft*, Band 5, Heft 3, Leipzig, 1926.

XLVII (4TH EDITION)

(*a*)

Authorities.—O, C[1], Bye, Ca, I, N, P[1111] identical. B, L, L[1], A nearly the same as the foregoing. W as text.

Know that thou shalt be separated from thy soul,
Within the veil of the secrets of God thou shalt go ;
Drink wine. Thou dost not know whence thou didst come.
Be content. Thou dost not know whither thou art going.

(*b*)

Authorities.—B[11], B[1111], Ca, N all identical. W as text.

Oh ! The long while that we shall be no more, and the world will exist ;
Without (remembrance of) our name, or sign, it will exist ;
Before this we were not—and no harm ensued ;
After this—when we exist no more—it will be just the same.

XXXVIII AND XLVIII

Authorities.—C[1], B, B[111], Bye, Ca, I, I[1], L, L[1], N, A are all identical. O, B[11], P[1], and P[1111] almost the same. R somewhat different. W as text.

This caravan of life passes in a wonderful manner,
Make the most of the moment that passes gaily ;
Why art thou disquieted about the morrow of thy friends ?
Set the cup before me—for the night passes.

XLIX (4TH EDITION)

(*a*)

Authorities.—C, C[1], B[11], B[1111], I, I[1], L, L[1], N, P[11111], A are identical. B[1] and Bye nearly similar. W as text.

From the halting place of infidelity to the faith is a single breath,
And from the world of doubt to certainty is a single breath ;
Treasure this single and precious moment,
For from the harvest of life—there is only this single breath.

(*b*)

Authorities.—O and P¹¹¹¹ identical. The " tashdid " over the " nun " in the word *laduni* " from on high " is, I think, an error. W as text.

> My heart said : " I long to learn the way (science) of inspiration,
> If thou art able instruct me."
> I said : " Alif." She said : " Say no more.
> If the Master is in the house, one letter (of his name) suffices."

LI (4TH EDITION)
(*a*)

Authorities.—The crux in this highly mystical quatrain lies in the first line between *máh* " moon " and *báda* " wine ". C, C¹, I, I¹ are identical and have " moon ". B¹¹¹, B¹¹¹¹, Bye, L, L¹, N, A vary and have " wine " in the first line. It seems that FitzGerald followed N and he translated the word " whose secret presence ", and this is undoubtedly what is meant. The text is taken from Bye and N, which are identical. W as text.

> That wine (mystic essence) that is by nature capable of change,
> Is sometimes an animal and sometimes a herb.
> Think not from this that it will cease to be. Away with such a thought !
> It is shown by its essence, though devoid of (permanent) character.

(*b*)

Authorities.—C, C¹, B¹¹¹¹, Bye, I, I¹, L, L¹, A are identical. N has l. 3 " Rise ! for the fire of youth is water." W as text.

> Put wine in my hand, for my heart is on fire,
> And this fleet-footed life is like quick-silver.
> Arise, for the waking (prosperity) of thy good luck is a dream.
> Know this : the fire of youth is (but) water.

FitzGerald's note.—From *Máh* to *Máhi*, from fish to moon.

Further note.—That is " universal ", the earth, according to the fable, being balanced on one horn of a bull, that is supported by a fish that swims in chaos. When the bull is tired he tosses the earth on to the other horn, and thus causes earthquakes.

LII (4TH EDITION)

Authorities.—L, L¹, A are identical. C, C¹, B¹¹¹, I, I¹, N are slightly different in l. 4. W as N.

> Sometimes hidden from view Thou showest Thy face to none.
> Sometimes Thou appearest in the forms of the world.
> Oh ! manifest Thy glory to Thyself,
> Thou art Thyself the perfection of manifestation, and Thou art Thyself the
>   spectator.

Note.—['ain-i-'aiyán. Perfection of manifestation.—W. H.]
This doctrine is one of those mysteries affected by certain Sufis, who hold that everything is a reflection of God's face. The late Professor Browne quoted Jámi's " Yusuf-u-Zulaika " in his book, *A Year Among the Persians*, as follows :—

> Beware ! Say not " He is all-Beautiful
> And we his lovers." Thou art the Glass
> And He the Face, confronting it which casts
> Its image on the mirror. He alone
> Is manifest, and thou in truth art hid—

and adds : So is it written in the Kurán *Kullu shaiⁱⁿ halikᵘⁿ illa wajhu-hu* " All things shall perish save His Face " (Kurán xxviii, 88). Compare also Kurán lviii, 3, " He is the first and the last ; the Seen and the Hidden."

LIII (4th Edition)

Authorities.—C, C¹, B, Bye, I, I¹, L, L¹, P¹, R, A (defective) are identical. N almost identical with the foregoing. W as N.

> If the heart understood the secret of life,
> In death also it would understand the secrets of God.
> To-day being thyself, thou didst know nothing,
> To-morrow, when thou leavest thy entity, what shalt thou know ?

XXXIX AND LIV

Authorities.—B¹¹¹, B¹¹¹¹, Bye, L, L¹, A (defective) are identical. O, P¹, P¹¹¹¹ have in l. 3 " Foolish one ! " W as text.

> Those who are the prisoners of intellect and discernment,
> Have come to nought, in vain wrangling about existence and non-existence ;
> Go ! Prudent one ! and choose rather the juice of the grape,
> For those fools from unripe grapes have become bitter.

Note.—A difficult quatrain. The following may throw some light on it. *Ghura* means unripe grapes ; *mawiz*, not *mawwiz*, means dried grapes ; but *mawiz db* means an acid and inebriating drink made from dried grapes and water, whence we may conclude that *mawiz* means dried grapes that are bitter.

XL AND LV

Authorities.—B¹¹, B¹¹¹, B¹¹¹¹, N are identical. C, C¹, B, B¹, Ca, I, L, L¹, P, P¹, P¹¹¹¹, A vary slightly. W as text.

> I will drink a one-man cup of wine
> (Then) I will enrich myself with two cups of wine ;
> First I will pronounce thrice my divorce from sense and faith,
> Then I will take the daughter of the grape to spouse.

Note.—[A man is a measure of weight, about 2 lb.—W. H.]

XLI AND LVI

Authorities.—L, L¹, N, P, P¹, P¹¹¹¹, R, A are identical. *Fardzdasti* in l. 2 of N is clearly a misprint for *faráz-u-pasti*. O is nearly similar. W as O.

> I know the outwardness of non-existence and of existence,
> I know the inwardness of all that is high and low,
> And yet I weary of my own concept
> If I acknowledge anything higher than inebriation.

FitzGerald's note.—A jest, of course, at his studies. A curious mathematical quatrain of Omar's has been pointed out to me ; the more curious because almost exactly parallel'd by some verses of Dr. Donne's that are quoted in Izaak Walton's Lives ! Here is Omar : You and I are the image of a pair of compasses ; though we have two heads (*sc.* our feet) we have one body ; when we have fixed the centre for our circle we bring our heads (*sc.* feet) together at the end." Dr. Donne :—

> If we be two, we two are so
> As stiff twin-compasses are two ;
> Thy soul, the fixt foot, makes no show
> To move, but does if the other do.

And though thine in the centre sit,
    Yet when my other far does roam,
Thine leans and hearkens after it,
    And grows erect as mine comes home.

Such thou must be to me, who must
    Like the other foot obliquely run ;
Thy firmness makes my circle just,
    And me to end where I begun.

LVII (4TH EDITION)

Authorities.—C, C¹, Ca, I, I¹, L, L¹, A are identical. B¹¹¹ has *miskín* for *lîkin* in l. 3, but is otherwise identical. Bye slightly different. W as text.

My enemy in error said that I was a philosopher ;
God knows I am not what he said I was.
But since I have come into this nest of sorrow,
I am, in a word, in a worse case : for I know not who I am.

XLII AND LVIII

Authorities.—C, Bye, I, I¹, N, A are identical. C¹, B¹¹, B¹¹¹, B¹¹¹¹, Ca, L, L¹, P¹, P¹¹¹¹, R also almost identical, have in the last line " drink wine and be quiet ". B is nearly similar. W as text.

Last night in drink I passed a tavern,
I saw a drunken old man with a vessel on his shoulder ;
I said : " Old man ! Art not thou ashamed before God ? "
He replied : " Mercy is from God ! Go and drink wine ! "

XLIII AND LIX

Authorities.—B, B¹¹, L, L¹, A are identical. O, C¹, B¹¹¹, Bye, Ca, I, N, P, P¹, P¹¹¹¹ vary slightly. W as N.

Drink wine, for it will banish excess (bigotry) from thee,
And will relieve thee from brooding on the seventy-two sects ;
Refrain not from an Alchemy of which
One draught will extinguish a thousand arguments.

FitzGerald's note.—The seventy-two religions supposed to divide the world, *including* Islamism, as some think, but others not.

Further note.—" Excess." Some commentators think bigotry is meant. Some translate '*illat* in the last line as " needs " or " calamities ". Nicolas translates *kímíái* " l'alchemie ou pierre philosophe ". As to the seventy-two sects (which with one true sect made the seventy-three) compare Háfiz, p. 122.

XLIV AND LX

There is no parallel in Omar Khayyám.

FitzGerald's note.—Alluding to Sultán Mahmud's conquest of India and its dark people.

Further note.—Mr. Heron-Allen attributes the inspiration of this quatrain to a passage in the apologue of Attár's *Parliament of Birds* and to the two last lines of the quatrain which is set opposite FitzGerald's quatrain xxxix of the 4th edition above.

LXI (4th Edition)

Authorities.—O, B, B^{111}, B^{1111}, I, P, P^1, P^{1111}, R, A are identical. C^1, B^{11}, L, L^1, N vary slightly. W as N.

> I drink wine, and everyone who is a worthy fellow like me drinks wine
> And my wine-drinking in his sight is venial.
> God knew of my wine-drinking from beginningless eternity;
> If I abstain His knowledge was ignorance.

Note.—This is one of the so-called " wandering quatrains " of Zukowski and is found in Tálib-i-Amuli. It is No. 141 in Zukowski's list. See Dr. Rosen's article in *Zeitschrift der Deutschen Morgenländischen Gesellschaft*, Band 5, Heft 3, 1926.

LXII (4th Edition)

Authorities.—B, B^{11}, Bye, I^1, L, L^1, P^1 are identical. C, C^1, I are nearly similar to the foregoing. A has ll. 2 and 4 transposed. R nearly as text. Not in W.

> They say : " Drink no wine—for thou wilt suffer for it.
> In the day of recompenses thou wilt be cast into the fire."
> This is so ; but more agreeable than the two worlds
> Is the moment when thou art elated with wine.

LXIV (4th Edition)

Authorities.—C, C^1, I^1, A are identical. B^{11}, Bye, I, L, L^1 are nearly similar and have in l. 4 *báz bagasht.* W as text.

> We wandered far past gates (of cities) and thro' deserts,
> In all quarters of the world we wandered in our wanderings.
> From no one that came from that road did we hear.
> A traveller never passed again on the road once travelled.

Note.—I used to take the view that *báz bagasht* in l. 4 was the better reading, and that the meaning was that " I never heard . . . that anyone past again on the road once travelled ", but the identical versions are against this reading.

LXV (4th Edition)

Authorities.—C, C^1, B^{111}, Bye, I, I^1, N are identical. B^1, B^{11}, B^{1111}, L, L^1, P^1, R, A vary slightly. W as text.

Those who comprehend all learning and letters
From the collection of their perfections became candles to their companions,
But have found no road out of this dark night.
They have told a tale and have fallen asleep.

Note.—The first line was thus translated for me by Sir Wolseley Haig, and a more competent authority it were vain to seek. This is the last quatrain in M. Nicolas' Teheran version, and is thought by some to be aimed at the Prophet of Islám.

LXVI (4th Edition)

Authorities.—O, P^{1111}, R are identical. Ca, L, P, A have *hukm* or *'ilm* in l. 2 instead of *rái.* P^1 has in l. 4 " The tablet and pen, and heaven and hell are thy *cheeks* ". W as text.

> On the first day, beyond the heavenly sphere, my soul
> Sought the tablet and pen and heaven and hell.
> Then the Preceptor with his infallible judgment said to me,
> " The tablet and pen and heaven and hell are within thee."

G

LXVII (4th Edition)

Authorities.—O, B, Ca, I^1, P^{1111} are identical. C^1, B^1, B^{111}, B^{1111}, Bye, I, L, L^1, N, P, R, A vary slightly. W nearly similar.

> The sky is a girdle from our worn-out lives,
> Jihun is a mark of our pure tears,
> Hell is a spark from our useless worries,
> Paradise is a moment out of our times of contentment.

Note.—Bye has in l. 4 *dari* and R has the same, and Dr. Rosen translates it "a window (giving a glimpse) of our happy moments".
"Jihun", the Amu or Ak Su (White River) Oxus.
P has in l. 2 "a mark of our *foul tears*".

XLV (1st Edition)

Authorities.—B, B^{111}, B^{1111}, Bye, I, I^1 are identical. C^1, N, P^1, A have in l. 3 *kand'at* instead of *kidmat*. L, L^1, R vary somewhat. W nearly similar.

> Listen to me! Cream of old friends!
> Fear nothing from this heaven without head or foundation.
> Sit in a corner of the court of steadfastness,
> And gaze upon the little sport that heaven makes.

XLVI AND LXVIII

Authorities.—Ca, L, L^1, N, P^1, A are identical and have *hairdnim* in both ll. 1 and 4. C^1 and I have *Khwdnim* in l. 1. The Ouseley version, P^{11}, P^{1111}, and R have *garddnim* "we revolve" in l. 4. W as O.

> This revolving sphere in which we stand bewildered,
> We know as the pattern of a magic-lantern.
> Know that the sun is the lamp and the world the lantern frame,
> We are like figures that in it are bewildered.

FitzGerald's note.—*Fdnus-i-Khiydl*, a magic lantern still used in India; the cylindrical interior being painted with various figures, and so lightly poised and ventilated as to revolve round the lighted candle within.

XLIX AND LXIX

Authorities.—O, C^1, B^{111}, B^{1111}, Bye, I, I^1, L, L^1, N, P, P^{1111}, R, A are identical, but L, L^1, N, A transpose ll. 1 and 2. B and B^{11} vary a good deal. P^1 has in l. 4 "to the box of labour". W as text.

> In reality and not by pretence
> We are the pieces and heaven the player.
> We play our little game on the board of existence,
> We went one by one to the box of nothingness.

L AND LXX

Authorities.—B, B^{11}, B^{111}, I, P^1, A are identical. C, C^1, B^{1111}, Ca, I, L, L^1 (defective), R all vary. P^{1111} has the rhyme in *gúi, magúi, púi,* and *úi*. W nearly as text.

> O thou who art gone to the club of fate like a ball!
> Go to the left and to the right; but say nothing;
> For He that threw thee down amidst the galloping,
> He knows, and He knows, and He knows, and He —

FitzGerald's note.—A very mysterious line in the Original. *O dánad, O dánad, O dánad, O* —, breaking off something like our wood-pigeon's note, which she is said to take up just where she left off.

Further note.—The last line should, I think, be : *U dánadu,* etc., where the *waw* is pronounced as part of the preceding word.

Moreover, in his note to the 1st edition, FitzGerald has correctly *U dánad,* etc., but later he changed this to *O dánad* according to the Indian pronunciation.

In the very ancient game of Polo called by the Persians " Clubs ", which is still played in all its ancient simplicity and with its ancient impetuosity in the Himalayas, and perhaps elsewhere, the ball is thrown in at right angles to the length of the ground, whence we get " left and right ".

In the works of Edward FitzGerald (Macmillan, 1903) there is a Persian sketch of a young Polo-player. On the top of this sketch a line of Háfiz (p. 280) is inscribed : " Sturdy Horseman. Welcome to the Field. Strike the ball."

LI AND LXXI

Authorities.—C^1, B, B^{111}, B^{1111}, Ca, I, I^1, L, L^1 are identical. N, A almost similar. O, P, P^1, P^{1111} are different and have " The pen was never content ", probably due to an original scribe's error. W as N.

There was a mark on the Tablet. It remained hidden.
The pen has always been content with the good and with the bad.
Within the limits of Fate He appointed what must be.
Our worrying and our struggles (against fate) are vain.

LII AND LXXII

(*a*)

Authorities.—O, L^1, N, P, P^{1111}, R, A are identical. C^1, B, B^{1111}, I (defective), P^1, have in l. 1 " Observe this till, *tába,* of the sky ". Bye and N are nearly the same as the text. W as text.

This vault of heaven is like an inverted cup.
In it all the intellectuals lie low.
Observe the friendship of the flask and cup,
They are lip to lip and between them blood has fallen.

Note.—The last two lines have no relation to FitzGerald's poem. Nicolas compares the flask and cup to two lovers, and says that blood is " un emblème de la haine la plus implacable ". But Sir W. Haig says there is no foundation for this statement.

(*b*)

Authorities.—O, L, L^1, P^1, P^{1111}, R, A are identical and have in l. 3 " in the way of reason ". C^1, B, B^{111}, B^{1111}, I, I^1, N are also identical and have in l. 3 " in the way of love ". W agrees with O, which was the source of FitzGerald's inspiration.

The good and the bad that are in the nature of man,
The joy and the sadness that belong to fate.
(As to these) do not attribute them to heaven—for in the way of reason
The heaven is a thousand times more helpless than thyself.

Note.—" The way of love " is difficult to understand. But the quatrain is mystical and Nicolas translates it : " Car cette roue, ami, est mille fois plus embarrassée que toi dans la voie de l'amour (divin)."

LIII AND LXXIII

(*a*)

Authorities.—B, L, L¹, P¹, P¹¹¹¹, A are identical. O and N nearly similar. R varies in l. 2. W as N.

> Dear heart ! Since the truth of the world is but pretence,
> Why art thou so overborne by this lengthy suffering ?
> Resign thyself to Fate, and adjust thyself to thy troubles,
> For the pen once gone forward will not come back for thy sake.

(*b*)

See against LXXI (4th Edition), " There was a mark, etc."

LXXIV (4TH EDITION)

(*a*)

Authorities.—O, C¹, I, P, P¹¹¹¹, R, A are identical. L, L¹ (defective) nearly similar. W as text.

> Be happy ! For they settled (cooked) thy sorrows yesterday,
> Secure from all thy vehement desires, yesterday.
> Live well content, for undisturbed by thy importunities, yesterday,
> They fixed, yesterday, what thou shalt do to-morrow.

Note.—" Cooked." Dr. Rosen translates " hart gebacken " as pottery is baked, and becomes *fixed.*

(*b*)

See against XLVII (4th Edition), last two lines of (*a*).

LIV AND LXXV

Authorities.—C, C¹, B¹¹, B¹¹¹, B¹¹¹¹, Bye, Ca, I, I¹, N are identical. L and L¹ (defective), A (defective), nearly similar. W as text.

> In that day when they saddled the horse of the heavens,
> And set forth the splendour of Jupiter and the Pleiades,
> This was our lot from the diwán of Fate ;
> What fault is ours ? They caused this to be our portion (kismat).

FitzGerald's note.—Parwin and Mushtari. The Pleiades and Jupiter.

LV AND LXXVI

Authorities.—B¹ and B¹¹¹, P¹ are identical. C, C¹, I, L, L¹, A vary a good deal. R nearly as text. Not in W.

> Since He himself was without beginning He created me,
> And first He taught me the lesson of love ;
> And then He made a filing of a scrap of my heart,
> A key to the treasuries of the pearls of reality.

Note.—" Reality ", the real world, as opposed to the imaginary world of Sufis, Dervishes, Kalandars, *et hoc genus omne.*
The expression *dur-i-m'ani* " the pearl of reality " is a very common one.

LVI AND LXXVII

Authorities.—O, B^1, B^{11}, B^{1111}, Bye, P^1, P^{1111}, R^1 are identical. C^1, B, I, I^1, N, P, A vary slightly. P is defective in l. 1. W as N.

If I divulge my secret (griefs) to Thee in a Tavern
It is better than that I pray without Thee towards the mihrab.
O Thou the first and the last of all thy creatures,
Burn me if Thou wilt (or) cherish me, if Thou wilt.

Note.—This is the second quatrain in the Ouseley MS. and in P^{1111}, and since it has been taken out of its proper place in the diwán, it would seem after the manner of Muslim poets to be propitiatory. These two versions have their first and second verses, both apologetic, the same.

The Mihrab is a niche in the wall of a mosque denoting the direction of Mecca, towards which the Muslims prostrate themselves in prayer.

LXXVIII (4TH EDITION)

(a)

Authorities.—C, Ca (defective), N are identical. C^1, B, B^{1111}, Bye, I, I^1, L, L^1, P^1 (defective), P^{1111}, A vary slightly. R differs somewhat. W as text.

When God mixed the clay of our existence,
He knew what the outcome of our actions would be.
Without his command there is no sin in me,
Then why did He wish to burn me at the resurrection?

(b)

Authorities.—B^{111}, Ca, L, L^1, N, A are identical. B, B^{11} vary. B^{1111} has in l. 2 *maguriz.* P^1, R^1 differ in l. 4 and have " This is as if He said slant the cup and yet no liquor spill ". P^{1111} also differs and has in l. 2 " In its contest with the soul how shall the body conquer ". W as text.

Thou hast issued a command from which to refrain is impossible,
And (nevertheless) ordered us to flee from it.
Therefore helpless between Thy command and prohibition,
We worldlings fail to carry out Thy order to slant the cup and yet no liquor spill.

Note.—This quatrain is one of Zukowski's so-called " wandering quatrains " and is found in Ni'amatulláh-i-Karmáni. It is No. 173 in Zukowski's list. See Dr. Rosen's article in the *Zeitschrift der Deutschen Morgenländischen Gesellschaft*, Band 5, Heft 3, 1926.

LXXIX (4TH EDITION)

Authorities.—B^{11}, Ca, L, A are identical. B^{111} almost exactly the same. C, C^1, I, L^1 vary. W as text.

While for the mould they mixed my clay,
Then (they caused) the resistance that they stimulated in my clay.
Better than I am I cannot be,
For thus they poured me out from the crucible.

Note.—The Calcutta version has in l. 2, " They produced a hundred wonders in me." The first line talks confusedly of " mixing " the mould instead of the clay. Nevertheless FitzGerald triumphed over such defects.

LVII AND LXXX

Authorities.—O and B (defective) are identical. N differs a good deal. W nearly similar to text.

> Thou settest snares on my path in a thousand places
> And sayest " I will catch thee if thou settest foot (in them) ".
> In no single thing is the world independent of Thy commands,
> Thou rulest everything and yet callest me " rebel ".

LVIII AND LXXXI

(*a*)

Authorities.—C, C^1, N are identical. B, B^1, B^{111}, Bye, Ca, I, I^1, L, L^1, P^1, P^{1111}, R, A vary very slightly without change of meaning. W as text.

> I am a sinful slave. How canst Thou be pleased with me ?
> My heart is darkened. Where is Thy light and purity ?
> If for Thy worship Thou givest me heaven,
> This is wages. Where are Thy favour and gift ?

Note.—This is one of Zukowski's so-called " wandering quatrains ". It is found in Abdulláh-i-Ansári and is No. 66 in Zukowski's list. See Dr. Rosen's article in the *Zeitschrift der Deutschen Morgenländischen Gesellschaft*, Band 5, Heft 3, 1926.

(*b*)

Authorities.—C, B^1, B^{111}, B^{1111}, Bye, Ca, L, L^1, N, A are identical. C^1, I are nearly similar. W as text.

> O Thou ! who knowest the secrets of the hearts of all,
> Helper of all in their helplessness ;
> O Lord ! give me repentance and accept my excuses,
> O Thou ! the giver of repentance, and the acceptor of the excuses of all.

(*c*)

Authorities.—C, B, Bye, Ca, I, L, L^1, N, R, A are identical. W as text.

> The manager of the affairs of the dead and living art Thou,
> The holder of this unstable wheel of heaven art Thou ;
> However bad I be, the Master of this slave art Thou,
> To whom shall sin be imputed, since the creator (of all) art Thou.

Note.—This is the second quatrain in the preface to Bye and has been taken out of its place in the diwán. Like that against lxxvii, 4th edition, it seems to be apologetic. Moreover, its genuineness is certain, for when Najmuddin Rázi attacked Omar Khayyám as an " unholy Philosopher, Atheist and Materialist ", he made use of this quatrain in his denunciation. See Dr. Rosen's article in the *Zeitschrift der Deutschen Morgenländischen Gesellschaft*, Band 5, Heft 3, 1926.

LIX AND LXXXII

LX AND LXXXIII

Authorities.—B^{11}, B^{111}, B^{1111}, Bye, Ca, L, L^1, N, A are identical. O, C^1, I, I^1, P, P^1 (defective), P^{1111}, R vary slightly. W as O.

Last night I was in the workshop of a potter,
I saw two thousand pots, some talking, some silent.
They all cried out to me in the language of their state (as pots)
" Where is the potter, and the pot-buyer and the pot-seller ? "

Note.—The third line of the Ouseley MS. reads " suddenly one of the pots shouted out ", and this is reflected in FitzGerald's paraphrase in LX, 1st Edition.

As to the potter and pots, cf. Kurán, s. xlviii, " He created man of clay like that of a potter."

LXI AND LXXXIV

Authorities.—Bye, Ca, I¹, R are identical. C, C¹, B, B¹¹, B¹¹¹, I, L, L¹, A vary slightly. W as text.

There is a cup that wisdom extolls,
And for love of it sets a hundred kisses on its brow.
Such a lovely cup this Potter of the world makes,
And then flings it down on the ground again.

LXII AND LXXXV

Authorities.—The different versions vary greatly. Ca, L (defective), L¹ (defective), R are identical. O, C¹, B, B¹¹¹, B¹¹¹¹, Bye, I, I¹, N, P¹, P¹¹¹¹, A all vary more or less. W nearly as N.

He who put together the pieces of a cup
Cannot permit his hand to shatter them.
Such heads and delicate hands who with his finger-tips
Combined ? And who from hate could shatter ?

Note.—This is one of Zukowski's so-called " wandering quatrains " and is found in Nasíruddin Túsí. It is No. 10 in Zukowski's list. Dr. Rosen, however, shows that Zukowski is in error in ascribing it to Nasíruddin Túsí, for the author of the history of the conquests of Changiz Khán speaking of the frightful slaughter of Merve mentions that Sayid 'Izzuddin, who with thirteen companions spent a day and a night on counting the dead, quoted this very quatrain. 'Aláuddin Malik-i-Juvaini wrote the history, Tarikh-i-Jahángushá, in A.H. 658, equal to A.D. 1260. See Dr. Rosen's article in the *Zeitschrift der Deutschen Morgenländischen Gesellschaft*, Band 5, Heft 3, 1926.

LXIII AND LXXXVI

Authorities.—I, I¹, L, L¹, P¹, R almost identical. C, C¹, B, B¹¹¹, B¹¹¹¹, Bye, A vary slightly. W as text.

When the Lord of the World arranged (human) natures,
Why did He thrust them into defect and waning ?
If the result was good, why break them ?
If not good, to whose fault are these forms attributable ?

Note.—In the Calcutta version the third line appears to be defective. Mr. Heron-Allen yokes this quatrain with LXXXVIII below. When Dr. Mingana discovered this verse as included in an Arabic MS. dedicated to a Persian author who died in A.D. 1282, a certain journal published in the United States of America acclaimed the discovery ; but without much cause. The quatrain was known to be genuine.

LXIV AND LXXXVIII

Authorities.—C, I, I¹ are identical. C¹, B, L, L¹, N are nearly similar to foregoing. P¹ and P¹¹¹¹¹ read "They say there will some talk in heaven". P¹¹¹¹¹ is defective. A has in l. 3 "But nothing but good can come from the resurrection". W as N.

> They say at the resurrection there will be a searching,
> And that beloved Friend will be hard-hearted.
> But from the perfect good, nothing but good can come.
> Be of good cheer. The end shall all be well.

Note.—The third line was quoted by the late Professor E. G. Browne in his disputes with modern Súfis. See *A Year Amongst the Persians*, p. 335, which I quote through the courtesy of Sir Denison Ross. This quatrain is a Persian version of an original Arabic verse of Shahrazuri. See Dr. Rosen's article in the *Zeitschrift der Deutschen Morgenländischen Gesellschaft*, Band 5, Heft 3, 1926.

LXV AND LXXXIX

Authorities.—O, P, P¹, P¹¹¹¹, A are practically identical. B¹¹, Bye, N are also identical and have in l. 2 "When at Death's hands like a fowl my feathers are plucked out". C¹, B, B¹¹¹, I, I¹, L, L¹, R vary. W as N.

> When I am thrown headlong under the foot of Death,
> And am rooted up from the hope of life,
> Beware, make nothing but a wine-jug from my clay;
> Haply when it is full of wine I may live again.

Note.—This quatrain is one of Zukowski's so-called "wandering quatrains", and is found in Háfiz. It is No. 220 in the list. See Dr. Rosen's article in the *Zeitschrift der Deutschen Morgenländischen Gesellschaft*, Band 5, Heft 3, 1926. We know, however, how constantly Háfiz borrowed from 'Omar.

LXVI AND XC

Authorities.—Ouseley only. W the same.

> The mouth of Ramazán has gone and Shawwál has come,
> The time of joy and pleasure and story-tellers has come;
> The time has come when with leather flasks on their shoulders they
> (The porters) cry: "Give way! The Porter has come."

Note.—This concludes the *Kúza-Náma* or "Book of Pots". FitzGerald's note on this subject follows. It was appended by him to quatrain LXXXVII (4th Edition) but seems to fit better the end of his *Kúza-Náma*.

FitzGerald's note.—The relation of Pot and Potter to Man and his Maker figures far and wide in the literature of the world, from the time of the Hebrew Prophets to the present; when it may finally take the name of *Pottheism* by which Mr. Carlyle ridiculed Stirling's *Pantheism*. My Sheikh, whose knowledge flows in from all quarters, writes to me :—

"Apropos of old Omar's Pots did I ever tell you the sentence I found in Bishop Pearson on the Creed? 'Thus are we wholly at the disposal of His will, and our present and future condition framed and ordered by His free but wise and just decrees. *Hath not the potter power over the clay, of the same lump to make one vessel unto honour, and another unto dishonour?* (Rom. ix, 21). And can that earth-artificer have a freer power over his *brother-potsherd* (both being made of the same metal) than God hath over him, who by the strange fecundity of His omnipotent power first made the clay out of nothing, and then made him out of that?'"

And again from a very different quarter. I had to refer the other day to Aristophanes, and came by chance on a curious speaking-pot story in the *Vespæ*, which I had quite forgotten :—

Φιλοκλέων.	Ακουε, μὴ φεῦγ᾽ εν Συβάρει γυνή ποτε l. 1435
	κατέαξ ᾽ἐχῖνον.
Κατήγορος.	Ταῦτ᾽ ἐγὼ μαρτύρομαι.
Φι.	Οὐχῖνος οὖν ἔχων τιν᾽ ἐπεμαρτύρατο
	Εἶθ᾽ ἡ Συβαρῖτις εἶπεν, εἰ ναὶ ταν κόραν
	τὴν μαρτυρίαν ταύτην ἐάσας, ἐν τάχει
	ἐπιδεσμον ἐπρίω, νουν ἄν εἶχες πλείονα.

The Pot calls a bystander to be witness to his bad treatment. The woman says : ' If, by Proserpine, instead of all this ' testifying ' (cf. Cuddie and his Mother in *Old Mortality* !) you would buy yourself a rivet, it would show more sense in you ! ' The Scholiast explains *echinus* as " ἄγγος τι ἐκ κεράμου."

One more illustration for the oddity's sake from the *Autobiography of a Cornish Rector* by the late James Hamley Tregenna, 1871.

"There was an old fellow in our company—he was so like a figure in the *Pilgrim's Progress* that Richard always called him the ' Allegory ', with a long white beard, a rare appendage in those days, and a face the colour of which seemed to have been baked in, like the faces one used to see on earthenware jugs. In our country-dialect earthenware is called ' Clome '; so the boys of the village used to shout out after him : ' Go back to the Potter, old Clome-face and get baked over again.' For the ' Allegory ', though shrewd enough in most things, had the reputation of being *saift-baked*, i.e. of weak intellect."

XC

FitzGerald's note to this quatrain. At the close of the Fasting Month, Ramazán (which makes the Mussulman unhealthy and unamiable) the first glimpse of the new moon (who rules their division of the Year) is looked for with the utmost anxiety and hailed with acclamation. Then it is that the porter's knot may be heard—toward the *cellar*. Omar has elsewhere a pretty quatrain about the same moon :—

> " Be of Good Cheer—the sullen Month will die,
> And a young Moon requite us by and by :
> Look how the Old one, meagre, bent, and wan
> With Age and Fast, is fainting from the sky ! "

LXVII AND XCI

(a)

Authorities.—C, C¹, B, I are identical. B¹¹¹, B¹¹¹¹, Bye, Ca, L, L¹, N, P¹, P¹¹¹¹, P¹¹¹¹¹, R, A vary slightly. B¹¹¹, L¹, P¹¹¹¹¹ have in l. 3 " If you wish to smell me ". W as text.

> When I am dead wash me with wine,
> Say my burial service with pure wine.
> If you wish to see me on the resurrection day,
> Seek me in the dust of the entrance to a wine-tavern.

(*b*)

Authorities.—O, P¹, P¹¹¹¹, R identical. C¹, B¹¹, B¹¹¹¹, Bye, I, I¹, L, L¹, N, P, A vary slightly. P reads in l. 1, " Stay me with the divining cup of Jamshid ". W as N.

> Take heed to stay me with the wine cup,
> And make this amber face like a ruby.
> When I pass away, wash me with wine
> And make my bier from wood of the vine.

LXVIII   AND   XCII

Authorities.—B¹¹, B¹¹¹¹, Bye, Ca, I, I¹ (defective), L, P¹¹¹¹, A are identical. C, C¹, B, L¹, N, R are almost the same as foregoing. W as N.

> So much wine will I drink that the perfume of wine
> Shall arise from the dust beneath which I lie ;
> So that when a toper shall pass by my grave,
> He shall become senseless from the scent of my earth.

LXIX   AND   XCIII

Authorities.—B, B¹¹, B¹¹¹¹, Ca, L¹, N are identical. C, C¹, B¹¹¹, Bye, I (defective), L, P¹, A vary and are nearly similar to foregoing. W as text.

> Since my nature was inclined to prayer and fasting,
> I said (to myself) a perfect salvation is assured to me.
> Alas ! that my ablution was spoilt by a gust of wind,
> And that fast was rendered vain by half a draught of wine.

LXX   AND   XCIV

Authorities.—B¹¹¹¹, Bye, Ca, L, L¹, A are identical. C, C¹, B, B¹, B¹¹¹, I, I¹ vary slightly. W as text.

> Every day I intend to do penance at night,
> Penance from cup and from goblet brimful :
> Now that the season of roses has arrived, grant me release,
> In the season of roses grant, O Lord, repentance for (intended) penance.

LXXI   AND   XCV

Authorities.—Ouseley alone has this quatrain in the form which was known to FitzGerald and is here given. The last two lines are found in a quatrain which is common to B¹¹, B¹¹¹, B¹¹¹¹, L, L¹, A in an identical form, and in C¹, I, and N in a form slightly varied, and reads :

> " Since Venus and the Moon became visible in the sky,
> No one ever saw anything better than wine of a ruby colour.
> I am astonished at the wine-sellers, etc., etc."

P, P¹, P¹¹ have l. 1 : " As long as the wheel of heaven has appeared in the sky." W as N.

> Although wine has rent my veil (of honour)
> As long as I live I will not part from wine.
> I am astonished at the wine-sellers, for what
> Shall they buy better than what they sell ?

LXXII AND XCVI

Authorities.—C, C¹, B, B¹¹, I, P¹¹¹¹, R¹ are identical. B¹¹¹¹ almost the same. B¹¹¹, L, L¹, N, A vary slightly. W as N.

> Alas! that the book of youth is folded up
> And this fresh purple Spring has become December.
> That bird of mirth whose name was "prime of life",
> Alas! I know not when he came, when he departed.

Note.—This quatrain stresses the *gradual* approach of old age.

XCVII

Authorities.—B¹¹¹¹, Ca, L¹ are identical. C, C¹, Bye, I, L, N, R¹, A vary very slightly; so also does W.

> Oh! Would there were a place where I might rest,
> That by this long road I might arrive (where I would be)!
> Would that after one hundred thousand years, from the heart of the earth
> We might hope to blossom above like the verdure.

Note.—This is the last quatrain but one in R¹ and L and L¹, and there is reason to think that it was actually the last of Omar's quatrains, and that the quatrain which FitzGerald has paraphrased :—

> "Oh! Thou who burn'st in Heart for those who burn, etc., etc.,"

which is shown as the last in the diwán, was written by some *unkind* critic.

XCVIII

Authority.—Nicolas only. W is identical.

> I would that God should alter this world,
> And that He should do it now, that I might see how He does it;
> That He would cross my name out of His roll,
> Or from His hidden place increase my daily means.

LXXIII AND XCIX

Authorities.—B¹¹¹, B¹¹¹¹, Bye, I, I¹, L, L¹, R are identical. C, C¹, B, N, A almost the same. P¹ has in l. 4 "That free from control thou mightest cause thy heart to attain its desire". W as text.

> If I like God could control the heavens,
> I would do away with the heavens entirely.
> Other heavens I would so construct *de novo*
> That freed from control thou shouldest easily attain the wish of thy heart.

LXXIV AND C

Authorities.—C (defective), B¹, B¹¹¹, Ca, I, I¹ are identical. O, B, B¹¹, Bye, L, L¹, N, P, P¹, P¹¹¹¹, R, A vary slightly. W nearly similar.

> Since no promise of a morrow is ever given to us
> Gladden for a moment me who am distracted.
> Drink wine, my Moon, by the light of the moon, for the moon
> Will shine time without end and not find us.

Note.—This quatrain is one of Zukowski's so-called "wandering quatrains" and is found in 'Attár. It is No. 2 in Zukowski's list. See Dr. Rosen's article in the *Zeitschrift der Deutschen Morgenländischen Gesellschaft*, Band 5, Heft 3, 1926.

LXXV AND CI

(*a*)

Authorities.—B¹, L, L¹, P¹, A are identical, R is almost exactly similar. O, N, P¹¹¹¹ nearly similar. W as text.

> My friends ! When you agree to meet together,
> And delight in one another's charms,
> And when the Sáki takes (round) the Magian wine,
> Remember a certain helpless one with a benison.

Note.—" Magian wine." See note to quatrain II above.

(*b*)

Authorities.—Ouseley and P¹¹¹¹ only. A variation of the last preceding quatrain. W as text.

> My friends ! When you meet together socially
> It behoves you not to forget your old friend ;
> When you quaff together the wine that is so wholesome
> And my turn comes—turn down (an empty cup).

Note.—In these two variations we have a picture of the convivial meetings at which we may reasonably assume that many of the poet's epigrams were given out. They were doubtless noted and stored in the memory of his friends.

FitzGerald makes the " Sáki " or cup-bearer a girl. Having regard to Eastern manners and the seclusion of womanhood I used to doubt whether he was correct, and I suppose many persons acquainted with Persian poetry must have doubted too. But Dr. Rosen throws some light on the question, for in his introduction to his translation of *The Quatrains of 'Omar Khayyám*, Methuen, London, 1930, he says : " In imitation of Arabic poetry, where the masculine sex is always used for the beloved, it has become customary in Persian verse to speak of the beloved as of a youth. But this may be looked upon as purely conventional."

A few more examples of quatrains which have nothing to do with FitzGerald's selection are added :—

(1)

Authorities.—This quatrain is taken from the oldest known collection of the quatrains of 'Omar Khayyám, namely from a collection of thirteen quatrains discovered in 1922 by the eminent scholar Mirza Muhammad Khán-i-Kazvini in a MS. written by the hand of the poet Muhammad bin Badr-i Jájarmí, A.H. 741 = A.D. 1340–1. C, C¹, B, B¹, B¹¹¹, Bye, I, I¹, L, L¹, R¹¹, A are identical.

> Since the cloud has washed the cheeks of the tulip at new year's day
> Arise and pour wine into the goblet speedily.
> For this verdure which is to-day the object of your admiration
> Will to-morrow spring from your dust.

Note.—This quatrain is taken from Dr. Rosen's admirable *Persian Edition of the Quatrains of 'Omar Khayyám*, Luzac, London, 1928. As shown above, I found this quatrain reproduced without any variation whatever in eleven versions later in date than R¹¹. The quatrain beginning *Abar dmad* opposite to Fitz-Gerald's quatrains xxii and xxiii is of the same family.

(2)

Authorities.—B¹¹, L, L¹, A identical B¹¹¹ differs somewhat. W as text.

To a duck said a fish in the burning heat
" Can it happen that water should return to a stream that has gone ? "
The duck said " When thou and I are cooked,
What matters it whether, after my death, it be the sea or the source."

Note.—[*Sardáb* " water-head " is the point in the river at which the irrigation channel (*juy*) is drawn off. The duck's meaning is : When we are dead and cooked it will matter nothing to us whether the water is at the source or whether it has reached the sea.—W. H.]

(3)

Authorities.—C¹, B¹¹, B¹¹¹, Bye, Ca, I, I¹, L, L¹, N, P¹, P¹¹¹¹, A are identical. B and R nearly similar. W as text.

He who planted the earth and sky and heavens,
Laid many a stain on the sorrowful heart.
Many lips like rubies and tresses like musk
In the hollow earth and chambered mould He laid.

Note.—" Tresses " in the Arabic dual signifying one on each side.
" Hollow earth," lit. drum of the earth.
" Chambered mould," lit. box of the mould.
In burying their dead the Muslim excavate a recess *in the side* of the grave of sufficient height to allow the corpse to sit up and answer questions put to it by the angels Nakir and Munkir.

(4)

Authorities.—C, B¹, B¹¹¹, B¹¹¹¹, I, I¹, L (defective), L¹ (defective) are identical. Bye, A nearly similar. B and R have in l. 1 " When the recompense of the six points will be paid ". W as text.

Sharr in l. 3 of L and L¹ is probably a slip of the pen for *hashar*.

In the day when the recompense of every attribute will be (paid)
Thy merit will be gauged according to the value of every attribute ;
Strive in beauty of character—or on the day of reward
Thy resurrection will be according to the form of thy attributes.

Note.—The late Professor E. G. Browne explained that according to the Sufi doctrine, in the purgatory known as " the world of similitudes ", the human soul takes a form corresponding to its attributes ; thus a greedy, gluttonous man takes the form of a pig, etc., etc. See *A Year Among the Persians,* where Professor Browne quotes this very quatrain.
Swedenborg, also according to Dr. Inge, the Dean of St. Paul's, believed that bestial livers would be re-born in the forms of the animals they resembled.

(5)

Authorities.—C¹, Bye, I, L, L¹, A are identical. B¹¹¹, B¹¹¹¹ almost the same. W is the same.

To-morrow when they give out the portion of the blessed
They will reserve a portion for me also, wretched wastrel that I am.
If I arise as " good ", they will reckon me amongst the good,
And if as " bad ", they will forgive me amongst the bad.

(6)

Authorities.—C, B, B¹, B¹¹¹¹, Ca, I, I¹, L¹, N, P¹, R, A are identical and have in l. 1 *naksh*, here " illusion ", or as Nicolas translates the word " phantasmagorie ". B¹¹ and B¹¹¹ also have *naksh* and are nearly similar. Bye and L have *nafs* " soul ". W has *nafs*.

Thou didst ask : " What is this illusion (unreal apparition) ? "
If I were to tell you the truth it would be a long tale.
It is an apparition that has come from the ocean,
And that then returns to the depth of the ocean again.

Note.—This is the essence of the Persian Súfism and also of the Indian Gnosticism. Cf. Kurán, s. lxxxiv, " He maketh alive and causeth to die and to Him shall you return " ; also s. xci, " Verily we are God's and to Him shall we return," a pious ejaculation in constant use.
The modern Súfis explain that as mist and rain arise from the ocean and again return to it, so is the course of the human soul. Compare also Merlin's riddling in Tennyson's *Coming of Arthur* :—

Rain, sun, and rain ! and the free blossom blows :
Sun, rain, and sun ! and where is he who knows ?
From the great deep to the great deep he goes.

(7)

Authorities.—C¹, B, I, L, L¹, N, P¹, A are identical. R nearly similar. P¹¹ is different and reads, l. 1, " I saw a bird sitting on the dome of Tús." P¹¹¹¹ is nearly the same as P¹¹, l. 4, " Where is the jewelled crown of Kaikáus ? " W as text.

I saw a bird sitting on the battlements of Tús,
Holding before it the skull of Kaikáus.
To the skull it was saying, Alas ! Alas !
Where is the clash of little bells, and the rolling of the large bell ?

Note.—" Tús," a town about 40 miles north-east of Naishápúr where 'Omar lived ; the modern Mashad.
Kaikáus. Darius the Mede.
[*Jaras* is the small globular bell, strings of which are tied round the necks of pack-animals. *Kús* is the large brass bell, a pair of which is hung from the loads of the leading animal of a caravan. The peculiarity of this quatrain is the association of *báng*, a word usually appropriated to the sound of the *kús*, with *jaras*.—W. H.]
Dr. Rosen is of opinion that this quatrain refers to the music played at noon in the *naqára-khána* over the gate of the Sháh's palace, as a sign of royal power. See Dr. Rosen's edition. P¹¹¹¹ has another version that refers to the town of R'ai and the disappearance from the world of Hátim Tai.

(8)

Authorities.—C¹ (defective), I, I¹ are identical. B¹¹¹, L, L¹, A nearly similar. W as text.

Thou Queen-like majesty ! in love for whom I am inebriated,
And by whose cruelty I was reduced from being a Knight to a Pawn !
When I failed in the play of the Bishop and the King,
I put my Rook in opposition to thy Rook, and was mated.

Note.—The word *rukh* in Persian means " castle " in chess and also " cheek ". He put his " castle " in opposition to her " castle " and his " cheek " against her " cheek " and was mated !

(9)

Authorities.—B, L, L¹, P are identical. R, A almost similar. W as text.

The rose said : " In the lawn I am Joseph of Egypt,
A costly ruby, with a mouth full of gold."
I said : " As thou art Joseph give me a sign."
The answer came : " Behold, my garment soaked with blood."

Note.—Cf. Gen. xxxvii and Kurán, s. lxxvii. The latter reads :—

> And they came at nightfall to their father weeping.
> They said : " O our Father ! Of a truth we went to run races
> And we left Joseph with our clothes, and the wolf
> Devoured him."

(10)

There is great diversity in this quatrain. I, I¹, L are identical. L¹, P, P¹¹¹¹ are also identical and in common with C, B¹¹¹, N have in l. 2, " Utterly destroy the foundations of prayer and fasting." B¹¹, B¹¹¹¹, Bye are nearly similar to the first group. A is quite different in l. 2. W as N.

As long as thou art able carry out the tradition of the vagabonds,
Utterly destroy the foundations of worldly plots.
Hear the word of 'Umar-i-Khayyám,
Drink wine, keep to the road, and do good.

Note.—" Worldly plots." Probably the way of Sufis, whom the poet denounced in other quatrains. This appears to have been a poetic " last will and testament ".

Remark the poet's name as in Persian—'Umar-i-Khayyám—and as correctly shown in the catalogues of the British Museum. The common Omar Khayyám is *really* " *barbarous* ".

" Keep to the road " as is the way of Dervishes. Nicolas translates " rob ", but if so how about " do good " ? It is probable that *rah mizan* which is translated " rob " should read *rah mirau*, that is, " keep to the road." Dr. Rosen thinks this quatrain genuine. See his article in the *Zeitschrift der Deutschen Morgenländischen Gesellschaft*, Band 5, Heft 3, p. 291.

For Product Safety Concerns and Information please contact our EU
representative GPSR@taylorandfrancis.com
Taylor & Francis Verlag GmbH, Kaufingerstraße 24, 80331 München, Germany

9 7 8 1 1 3 8 0 6 1 0 6 4